GRACE-BASED RECOVERY

GRACE-BASED RECOVERY
A Safe Place to Heal and Grow

Jonathan Daugherty

New
Growth
Press
WWW.NEWGROWTHPRESS.COM

New Growth Press, Greensboro, NC 27404
www.newgrowthpress.com
Copyright © 2018 by Jonathan Daugherty

Cover Design: Faceout Books, faceoutstudio.com
Interior Typesetting and eBook: Lisa Parnell, lparnell.com

ISBN: 978-1-948130-11-0 (print)
ISBN: 978-1-948130-12-7 (ebook)

Printed in the United States of America

25 24 23 22 21 20 19 18   1 2 3 4 5

This book is dedicated to every person who has
the courage to step into a recovery environment.
May you discover God's grace in these pages—
how much he loves you and the new life
of freedom and peace he offers you.

CONTENTS

A Word to Group Leaders

As you endeavor to lead a recovery group, I commend you for taking on such a courageous and generous role. To help you get the most out of *Grace-Based Recovery* as a resource, I want to share a few things about the goals and emphases of a grace-based group, the best way to structure the group time, and the lesson format.

GROUP GOALS AND EMPHASES

Grace-Based Recovery is ultimately a guide to understanding and applying the truth of God's grace to overcome addictions and strongholds of any kind, and to live out the abundant life available in Christ. Every lesson is an opportunity to point group members to Christ, so they might experience his grace and power firsthand. Apart from Christ, we can do nothing (John 15:5b).

With that in view, before you begin, be sure that you and the group members have read *For Group Members: Before You Get Started*:

- How to receive God's gift of grace;
- What grace-based recovery is *not*; and
- Why grace is the best environment for recovery.

These will lay the foundation for understanding and applying the principles in each lesson.

YOUR ROLE AS LEADER

You don't need to have a history of addiction to be a group leader, but it is helpful if you can identify with the struggles of the group members. Always avoid creating any kind of "us vs. them" mentality between addicts and non-addicts. God's Word reminds us that *all* have sinned and fallen short of God's glory (Romans 3:23). Even if you have not committed the same sins as another group member, you are in as much need of grace as they are. Lead from such a position of humility.

GROUP GROUND RULES

As you begin, it's important to establish some basic ground rules for the group and your times together. Don't be afraid of having rules in a grace-based group. Grace isn't opposed to structure! Here are some basic rules to guide the group time:

- We protect confidentiality. We do not share someone else's story outside the group. We build trust by being trustworthy.
- We listen carefully. We don't interrupt or grab attention by inserting jokes.
- We don't talk too long. We make room for those who speak up less often.
- We understand that advice is not always welcome. We offer feedback only when invited to do so.
- We abide by the Golden Rule, treating others as we want to be treated.
- We remind each other of these rules whenever necessary.

Group meetings should take between sixty and seventy-five minutes. Group members are encouraged to do some homework between lessons that shouldn't take more than thirty to forty minutes to complete. Remind group members that what they will receive from the lessons is related to the investment of time and energy they will put in.

LESSON FORMAT

Each lesson follows this basic format:

Main idea (short paragraph)
Bible passage

Article (800-1000 words)
Discussion questions (3-5)
Group exercise

LEADER GUIDE

A Leader Guide is included in the back of the book for each lesson and contains notes with instructions on how you might deliver the content of the lesson and facilitate group discussion. Headings that are in all capital letters (SETUP, ASK) in most cases contain content that you can use to lead the discussion with your group. The notes after Leader guide are comments intended for you, as a way to orient you to the lesson themes and ideas and to provide hints and suggested answers to questions. These notes are not intended to be rigidly prescriptive. Feel free to let your personality and strengths shine as you consider the suggestions offered.

May God bless you as you lead fellow strugglers to Jesus Christ, the only One capable of bringing the dead back to life!

For Group Members: Before You Get Started

HOW TO RECEIVE GOD'S GIFT OF GRACE[1]

> For God so loved the world, that he gave his only Son, that whoever believes in him should not perish but have eternal life. For God did not send his Son into the world to condemn the world, but in order that the world might be saved through him. (John 3:16-17)

The foundation of grace-based recovery is *God's* grace. But what is God's grace and how can you receive it?

Simply put, God's grace is his undeserved kindness shown to all humanity. But there is a difference between what we might call God's "common" grace, extended to everyone, and his "saving" grace. The breath you are breathing is because of God's common grace. God is the Creator of all things, and all things benefit from God's common grace. But even though all creatures experience the beauty and benefit of God's creation, not all human beings experience his saving grace. That is, not all people have a personal relationship with God.

When God created the world, there was no sin or imperfection in it. He placed the first two humans, Adam and Eve, in the creation to care for and manage it (Genesis 2). God intended human beings to bear his image throughout the world as living reflections of their Creator (Genesis 1:26-28). In order for this relationship between God and humans to be one of love and not duty, God gave Adam and Eve free will, the ability to choose. And then he gave them a boundary, or a law.

---

1. For a more thorough exposition of the gospel, get the book *Free and Clear: Understanding and Communicating God's Offer of Eternal Life* by R. Larry Moyer (Grand Rapids: Kregel Publications, 2009).

God told Adam that there was one tree that he and Eve were not to eat from. If they did, they would die (Genesis 2:16-17). One day God's enemy, Satan, appeared to Adam and Eve and tempted them to cross the boundary that God had established (Genesis 3:1-5). They crossed that line and ate the fruit that God had forbidden. This one act of disobedience ushered sin into the world and brought with it the penalty of death and decay, both physically and spiritually. Immediately, Adam and Eve were spiritually separated from God because of their sin (Genesis 3:6-24). Their relationships were broken, with God and with each other.

This condition of brokenness and separation from God continues with every generation. Humans are born with sin in their essential nature, a hard-wired desire to disobey God. This is why it comes so naturally to break God's laws (by lying, stealing, cursing, committing adultery, coveting, etc.). And nothing we do can earn our way back to the pure, undefiled relationship with God that Adam and Eve had at the beginning, before they sinned (Romans 3:10-20). We are truly trapped and lost in our sin (Ephesians 2:1-3).

But God did not abandon Adam and Eve. He also didn't abandon you or me. He made a promise from the very beginning that he would provide a Savior for us, one who would defeat Satan's plan to destroy us and pay the debt that we, as sinners, owe God for breaking his law (Genesis 3:15, 21).

In the Old Testament, we see God institute his law (Exodus 20:1-17) and raise up priests and prophets who would call people to turn from their sin in repentance and turn to God in faith. At that time, God required the blood sacrifice of animals to be offered as payment for the sins of his people. But these rituals had to be done over and over again because no animal could fully satisfy the debt owed to God for sin. Only a sinless human being could satisfy the demands of God's justice (Hebrews 9:11-28).

Enter Jesus Christ. He was the promised Savior. He was born of a virgin; his Father was God—and he himself was God. Both fully God and fully man, he was able to live a sinless life—the life we are unable to live—even as he faced every temptation that we face as human beings. He was "God in the flesh" and the only one able to satisfy the Father's righteous judgment against sin.

Jesus performed miracles to prove that he was God, sent from heaven by his heavenly Father and anointed by him to be the promised Savior. He stopped storms with his words. He raised men from the dead. He healed the lame, sick, and blind. And he shared the Good News of God's salvation through faith—faith in him.

But Jesus's work of salvation was not performing miracles. Jesus came to earth to pay the debt that you and I owe to God for our sin. Every human being stands under God's judgment as a sinner. We owe God for the sins that we have committed against him. But we can't pay what we owe. God demands a payment of sinlessness or perfect righteousness—something that you and I don't possess. This is why Jesus is the critical link for us.

Jesus lived the perfect, sinless life. But death is the penalty for our sin. So Jesus needed to pay that penalty to erase our debt. On our behalf, as our perfect substitute, Jesus died on a cross, bearing the sins of the world. He physically died, carrying the weight of every human being's sin in all of history, past and future (including yours and mine). Because he took our punishment and paid our penalty, our sins can be forgiven, no longer held against us by God when we put our faith in Christ's work on our behalf.

Yet there is more! But God desired more than just our debt being paid. God wants us to have life—eternal life.

Therefore, on the third day after Jesus died, he rose from the grave, and he offers new, eternal life to all who trust in him. He showed himself to hundreds of his followers over a period of forty days before ascending back to heaven. He conquered sin and death, and now offers the free gift of forgiveness and eternal life to anyone who trusts in him alone for salvation. This is God's saving grace.

Jesus said, "I am the way, and the truth, and the life. No one comes to the Father except through me" (John 14:6). The only way you can know the fullness of God's grace and have a relationship with him is to have faith in Jesus Christ—to trust that Jesus is God's promised Savior and that through him you are forgiven and restored.

Do you want to receive the fullest expression of God's grace through faith in Jesus Christ? Then let me invite you to pray to God. The following prayer may be used as a guide. It isn't the words printed below that save you. It is placing your trust in Jesus Christ alone as your only hope of being eternally joined with God.

> Dear God,
>
> Thank you for not giving up on me. I know that I am a sinner and that I have broken your law. I know that such disobedience deserves death, to be separated from you forever. But you made a way for me to be forgiven and restored to you through faith in your perfect Son, Jesus Christ. I place my trust right now in Jesus Christ alone as my only hope of salvation from the just penalty of my sin. Please fill me now with your life and help me to experience the abundance of your grace.
>
> Thank you for your love and kindness. Help me to grow in my relationship with you. I want to live according to your Word from this day forward.
>
> Amen.

If you just trusted in Jesus Christ for your salvation, I encourage you to tell someone. If you are part of a grace-based recovery group, share this experience with your group leaders. They will want to celebrate this pivotal moment in your life with you and help you begin to grow in your faith.

If you have further questions about the Bible and Christianity, seek out a local Christian church or visit Ligonier.org.

WHAT GRACE-BASED RECOVERY IS *NOT*

> For the grace of God has appeared, bringing salvation for all
> people, training us to renounce ungodliness and worldly pas-
> sions, and to live self-controlled, upright, and godly lives in the
> present age . . . . (Titus 2:11-12)

Grace is not weak. Quite the contrary—it is powerful! Just look at these
verses in Titus. It doesn't say that it is the law of God that trains us, or our
strong will, or the right curriculum. No, it says that it is *grace* that trans-
forms people from lives of ungodliness and worldly passions to lives that
are self-controlled, upright, and godly. Grace!

Sometimes people have misconstrued grace-based recovery, believing that
we think acting out is okay and that there shouldn't really be any accountability; believing that it is all about feeling good and making people happy.
Gag! Grace doesn't teach that.

If you are in a group that claims to be "grace-based" but never corrects or
challenges anyone who is repeatedly acting out or getting worse in their
addiction, then you need to flee that group as quickly as possible. Grace
is not an abandonment of the truth. One of the foundations of a healthy
recovery is brutal honesty, with ourselves and with each other. Don't join
any type of recovery program that pits grace and truth against each other.
They are not opposites; they exist in harmony.

Jesus was described as being full of grace and truth (John 1:14). This didn't
mean that he was full of grace one day and truth the next. He was full of
grace *and* truth, not grace *or* truth. This means that he told the truth within
the context of love and compassion for others. Whether he was chewing
out a religious leader for self-righteous duplicity or showing mercy to a
woman caught in adultery, he never compromised on the truth or on his
free gift of kindness to the undeserving.

The following will help you understand what grace-based recovery is *not*, so that you can better recognize what it *is* throughout the main lessons in the book.

Grace-based recovery does not say it is okay to keep acting out

When you begin to understand God's grace (his undeserved gift of kindness offered in Jesus Christ), there is a profound alteration in your perspective on acting out. You realize that God has withheld his just punishment for your sins and instead poured out the riches of his kindness. Why would you want to continue acting out when such grace has been given?

Grace does not teach us to say no to temptation in order to receive more grace, as if our doing the right thing earns us more grace. Grace is free! What grace teaches is that because we are *already* accepted and loved, we are really free to say no to sin. We don't have to perform to validate our worth. We can live free because we *are* loved, not in order to *be* loved.

I realize that even those who understand this truth about grace have still had plenty of experiences where acting out continued. But this doesn't diminish grace. It simply means that grace was not fully embraced at that point so that it impacted experience. It was only acknowledged intellectually.

There are many in recovery who have all the "right answers" but continue to live in ways contrary to those answers. Remember, though, that it is grace that trains us to say no; it's not the ability to spout off a bunch of great solutions. As God's grace moves deeper into your soul, you become more willing to give up your "answers" in favor of asking more questions—questions that reveal the true state of your heart and move you toward real healing and growth.

Grace-based recovery is not a celebration of sickness or depravity

Some might assume that because a person is encouraged to share their full story of brokenness, this opens the door for admiring, or even promoting, such behaviors. That simply isn't true. Occasionally, someone might start to "relive" their past while telling their story, in which case it is important for whoever is listening to step in and remind the person that sharing their story is for the purpose of confession and healing, not glorification of evil.

Those listening to someone share their story also need to be careful, protecting themselves from the temptation to lust or to encourage more detail than necessary. The goal of an addict telling their story is to remove all secrets from the darkness. If addicts do not get their story out into the light, they will never experience the fullness of true freedom. Grace allows for deep secrets to be exposed without shame.

Grace-based recovery is not a sin management system

Most recovery programs are oriented toward modifying behavior with a little emotional and spiritual work tossed in on the side. But mostly, they are about cleaning up behavior. This typically leads to a rigid performance-based system that, at best, can only teach a person to manage the addiction, not break free from it.

> For freedom Christ has set us free; stand firm therefore, and do not submit again to a yoke of slavery. (Galatians 5:1)

Behavior modification works for what it is designed to do: modify behavior! But there are lots of problems with this approach when it comes to helping addicts break free from deeply embedded compulsions. First, since it is only focused on behavior, it completely misses dealing with a person's heart. This is unfortunate because the only way an addict can truly break free from addiction is through the transformation of the heart. Behavior modification is primarily concerned with the addict not acting out.

Another problem with behavior modification is that it sets up an addict to form a belief system that is false: that freedom from addiction occurs from the outside in. In other words, if you get the external behaviors right, your heart will change too. Of course, this isn't true, but addicts who adopt behavior modification as the means to recovery will inevitably learn to believe this.

Finally, behavior modification can actually lead an addict *back into their addiction*! Yes, you read that right. When the addict's success or failure in recovery is measured solely by whether they have or have not acted out, they will eventually be forced to make a very tough decision: tell the truth or lie. Most choose to lie, which carries them right back to their old patterns of addiction.

"But why would they lie?"

Because they are being measured by their behavior, not by their intrinsic, unchangeable worth as a human being. And because behaviors are not static, the way they view their worth will be on a yo-yo. One day they might feel great about themselves because they are "behaving," but then the next day they feel horrible because they are not. That is not grace-based recovery.

Grace-based recovery is not easy

Contrary to what some might believe about grace-based recovery, it is not an easy path. Receiving grace is not comfortable; it challenges your pride and invites you to humble yourself, which most people are not good at doing. (Myself included!)

Over the years, we have had plenty of people abandon our groups and our programs, not because what we offered was too easy, but because they found grace-based recovery too hard! It is hard to let go of pride, legalism, control, and shame, and then embrace the gift of grace, walking into (not away from) inner brokenness, and committing to total transparency.

Do not be deceived into thinking that grace-based recovery is easy. It is not. It is much easier to embrace a recovery program of rigid rules, rituals, and behavior modification methods. You can feel justified and "accomplished" in such programs. They appeal to your pride and desire for control, all the while allowing you to ignore your deep brokenness. Yes, that is much easier, but it isn't that dissimilar to addiction. Only the context has changed.

Unfortunately, taking the easy road in recovery never leads to freedom. And I hope it is freedom that you actually want, whatever the cost. I can testify from personal experience that although grace-based recovery is not easy, it is worth it because of where it will take you. Grace-based recovery leads to places you cannot find through rules alone or behavior modification. Places like peace, joy, freedom, and an unwavering assurance that you are a beloved child of God.

WHY GRACE IS THE BEST ENVIRONMENT FOR RECOVERY

The heart, not behavior, is at the heart of recovery. This is very hard for many people to accept, whether those in recovery or those leading recovery programs. And even if this truth is acknowledged on an intellectual level, it is extremely difficult to embrace on an emotional one. It just seems way more obvious that behavior should be the primary focus of recovery.

The problem, however, with focusing on behavior in recovery is that it keeps the addict in a performance orientation rather than a relational one. If recovery is about changing the heart, then focusing on behaviors keeps the addict from ever reaching his or her heart. Everything can just stay up in the head. But a "heady" recovery is no real recovery at all.

Grace fosters an environment of love, which doesn't always translate to addicts immediately cleaning up their behavior. But it does lay the foundation for long-term transformation. Love is the best long-term motivator in recovery. Fear and rigid rules may whip an addict into clean behavior, but they cannot change the heart. That requires love.

When I began my recovery, I assumed (like every other addict) that all I needed was better behavior. I knew deep down that there was a mess in my soul, but I thought that if I could just learn to control my out-of-control behaviors, my heart would clean up too.

I was shocked to discover that better behavior did not have the magical effect on my heart that I assumed it would. In fact, the more I cleaned up my behavior, the more disconnected I felt from my heart! How could this be?

On one hand, I felt good that I wasn't acting out (as much). On the other hand, I felt hollow, still broken, and very detached from a part of me that had yet to wake up. My heart was still very much outside my recovery equation. Many in recovery today are in the same boat; clean on the outside, but broken and empty on the inside. Grace is the best environment for recovery because it allows you to be broken on the journey.

The goal of recovery is still healing and growth, but by taking the emphasis off behavior and placing it on your heart, you are free to experience full recovery, not simply behavioral recovery. And isn't that what you want, anyway? A full recovery? It's what I wanted.

If someone asked me now whether I would want cleaned-up behaviors within three months or a completely transformed life within ten years, I would take the ten years in a heartbeat. But too many in recovery are looking for a quick fix, an immediate change to make them feel better. And it's okay to want to feel better! But true recovery takes time. There is no such thing as a "quick fix" for addiction.

Recovery is a journey marked by numerous failures; each one a new opportunity to learn and grow. Grace gives you that opportunity. If you fall, get back up and learn from it. No penalties, no punishment, no shame. Get back up and take another step. If you fall on that step, get up. And the next one? Get up again.

> . . . for the righteous falls seven times and rises again . . . (Proverbs 24:16a)

Even the righteous fall. Nobody is failure-free, whether a recovering addict or a faithful saint. So the focus in recovery had better not be on whether or not you fall. We all fall! The focus needs to be on encouraging one another to "rise again." Grace creates the best environment for such encouragement.

Introduction

Grace-Based Recovery: A Safe Place to Heal and Grow

Main idea: Creating a safe, healing environment

Bible passage: Matthew 11:28-30

GBR article: A safe place to heal

Discussion questions

Group exercise

MAIN IDEA

Grace-based recovery is about creating a safe, healing environment for overcoming addictions and strongholds[1] of any kind. The atmosphere of a grace-based environment is welcoming and open, inviting broken sinners to find their hope and healing in Jesus Christ, not in the strength of their own will.

---

1. When the term "addiction" is used in this study, it primarily refers to compulsive, destructive behaviors. When the term "stronghold" is used, it primarily refers to spiritual and emotional bondage to false beliefs about yourself, God, and life.

BIBLE PASSAGE

Matthew 11:28-30

"Come to me, all who labor and are heavy laden, and I will give you rest. Take my yoke upon you, and learn from me, for I am gentle and lowly in heart, and you will find rest for your souls. For my yoke is easy, and my burden is light."

Introduction

A Safe Place to Heal

> "Hi. Welcome to the group. My name is Jonathan."
>
> "Hi. I'm Joe."
>
> "I'm glad you're here, Joe. We'll get started in a few minutes. Help yourself to some coffee and grab a seat in the circle. Hey guys, this is Joe."
>
> In unison, "Hi, Joe!"

If you are Joe, this can be a terrifying experience, right? On the one hand, it is wonderful to be greeted, reassured that you are in the right place, and actually welcomed. On the other hand, it is frightening because everybody knows why you are there. You are addicted. Ouch!

As scary as this scene may be, you must enter it if there is going to be any hope for freedom from your addiction. You must enter a place where you are accepted in all your brokenness, a place where healing is available and transformation is waiting. You must *enter*.

Grace-based recovery is a safe place

Grace-based environments often come in the form of a support group or small-group counseling or coaching. They are places where your full story can be heard without judgment or shame. In such an atmosphere, you are loved and embraced because of your *presence*, not because of your *performance*. It is safe to be real in a grace-based group.

Grace is an often misunderstood and misapplied concept. **Grace is simply defined as undeserved favor or kindness.** When you are offered grace, it is a free gift of acceptance and kindness that is not dependent on your goodness or behavior. It is a gift that validates your worth as a human being *because you are a human being.*

When you step into a grace-based recovery environment for the first time, it might feel a bit awkward, like you are in a foreign country. Is it really a place where you aren't condemned? A place where your worth isn't based on your performance? A place where joy, truth, and acceptance are offered with no strings? I know it seems too good to be true. It *is* good, but it's also true—grace is out there!

> "Joe, why don't you share some of your story with us? Tell us why you're here."
>
> "Well, are you sure you want to hear it? I mean, it's pretty bad. I've done some really stupid, hurtful things that I'm ashamed of. Is it really okay to share that here?"
>
> "Joe, we like to call this a 'No Shame Zone' (or NSZ for short). That means that no matter what you share, we won't stand in condemnation over you. Heck, we're just like you! We want you to share your story because until you do, you won't be able to start the journey of recovery to a whole new you."
>
> "Okay. Here goes . . ."

The foundation of a grace-based recovery environment is the invitation from Jesus in Matthew 11:28, "Come to me, all who labor and are heavy laden, and I will give you rest." This invitation is a call to both the self-righteous do-gooder and the desperate outcast to make their way to Jesus. In Jesus, there is rest for the weary; his grace invites you into his rest. And no one needs grace and rest more than the one who is addicted.

Do you want rest for your weary soul? Do you want a place where you can heal and grow? Then you need grace-based recovery, a place where your value is constant and your life matters to God. Take on the easy yoke and light burden of Jesus and you will discover the rest he promises.

Grace-based recovery is a healing place

Grace-based recovery means learning how to live in freedom every day. No one will do recovery perfectly, but perfection isn't the point. Healing and growth are what this journey is all about. Grace is the vehicle that moves you from a self-centered addict to a loving child of God.

Attitude in recovery is huge. Grace offers a vision of hope. No matter how far you have fallen in your addiction, grace always meets you there to pick you up. When you know that you have value, that *you are worth recovery*, you just might be able to take that first step and tell your story. You just might be able to start seeing yourself a little differently than before. You might start recovering and establishing a foundation for a whole new life.

If I gave you an acorn and told you to plant it today, would you expect to see a full-grown oak tree tomorrow? Of course not! There is a (long) process of growth that must occur before a tiny acorn becomes a massive oak. But the ultimate purpose of that acorn was always to become an oak tree. In the same way, your ultimate purpose has always been to be an "oak of righteousness" that bears God's holy image in his world (Isaiah 61:1-3). The seed of grace planted in you today will mature over time into a flourishing life of freedom and joy.

Grace-based environments give you the time and space to "grow up" in recovery. It takes time to unpack your whole story and start moving in a new direction. You need an environment where such time and patience are offered. That is grace-based recovery.

> "Joe, I sure hope we see you again soon."
> "Oh, I'm sure I'll be back. This is the best I've felt in years."
> "Well, just so you know, even if we don't see you for another six months, you're still welcome here. You are always welcome here."

DISCUSSION QUESTIONS

1. How can you identify with Joe's experience of stepping into a group for the first time? Why is a grace-based environment so important in that first encounter?

2. In a grace-based environment "you are loved and embraced because of your *presence*, not because of your *performance*." How does this idea make you feel? How does such an environment motivate you toward recovery?

3. What might make it difficult to enter a grace-based recovery environment?

4. How does a grace-based recovery environment change your perspective on the time frame it might take for real change and transformation to take place in your life? Does this encourage or discourage you? Why?

5. Is anything preventing you from coming to Jesus to find rest? If so, what is it? What would it take for you to let it go?

Introduction

Celebrate God!

Since this is a NSZ (No-Shame-Zone), share any fear you have about opening up to others about your weaknesses and failures. After each person shares, other members of the group are invited to make one affirming comment to the person who shared. (Be respectful, brief, and non-preachy.)

If you prefer not to participate verbally, simply say "Pass" when it is your turn. But consider allowing other members to speak affirming words over you, whether or not they know your specific fears. The truth spoken over you is powerful in breaking spiritual and emotional strongholds and affirming God's message of grace and love.

Lesson

1

Grace to Overcome

Main idea: Grace-based paradigm vs. performance-based paradigm

Bible passage: Titus 2:11-14

GBR article: Grace changes everything!

Discussion questions

Group exercise: Celebrate God!

MAIN IDEA

Grace is essential for overcoming addictive strongholds—the compulsive behaviors and false beliefs that have ensnared you. The fact that God offers you grace shows you that you have value to God; it's a value that isn't based on your performance. Grace is God's unearned favor or kindness toward you. You and I don't deserve God's love, but he offers it to us by grace. Therefore, recovery is more of a gift from God than it is a reward for your good performance.

Real recovery isn't just about *not* doing something wrong or unhealthy; it's about living daily in connection with God and others, and learning to live according to his Word. It isn't based on your skill or willpower; it's based on the grace of God. You must receive this gift of grace[1] and let it work in your life if you are ever to break free from addictive strongholds.

BIBLE PASSAGE

Titus 2:11-14

> For the grace of God has appeared, bringing salvation for all people, **training us to renounce ungodliness and worldly passions, and to live self-controlled, upright, and godly lives in the present age,** waiting for our blessed hope, the appearing of the glory of our great God and Savior Jesus Christ, who gave himself for us to redeem us from all lawlessness and to purify for himself a people for his own possession who are zealous for good works. (author's emphasis)

---

1. See "For Group Members: Before You Get Started" to learn how you can receive God's free gift of grace and eternal life.

1

ARTICLE

Grace Changes Everything!

Recovery from any addiction is hard. (What an understatement, right?) But sometimes it is made even harder by programs intended to help you break free from your compulsions. Some programs can make you feel as if an additional burden is being laid onto your already heavy heart. And even if a program is well-meaning, the message that can be communicated is, "If you don't measure up to the standards of our program, you will be seen as an even greater failure." This doesn't make for a good start to an already daunting journey.

Grace offers a different approach to recovery, one that doesn't place your value on the ever-changing roller coaster of performance. Grace gives hope to the person just realizing the need for recovery, and also breathes new life into the one who has been on the journey a while but feels stuck in a rigid rut of rules and performance-based rituals.

Grace-based recovery offers a pathway to true healing and lifelong freedom. Such recovery isn't merely about managing behaviors or simply "not acting out." It provides a way to experience fullness in every aspect of life and a pursuit of purpose that is meaningful and joyous.

I have experienced many different kinds of recovery programs since 1999, when all my secrets[2] and lies came to the surface. I have tried many methods,

---

2. Read my full story in my book, *Secrets* (NewGrowthPress.com/Secrets).

from "pain therapy" to intense Bible study and militaristic accountability.[3] I have read many books, worked with numerous counselors, attended seminars, and studied multiple curriculums on addiction recovery.

Over all these years, I have found very few, if any, resources that are grace-based. Most are what I refer to as "sin management systems," a way to feel better about yourself and your failures without ever truly breaking free. It is sad. But it is not unfixable!

Do you want to be free from your addiction? Of course you do! Addiction sucks. Literally. It sucks the life from you. It tears apart relationships, destroys character, weakens the body, depresses the soul, and ultimately leads to death—in all areas of life. *No one sets out to become addicted.* But once you find yourself drowning in addiction, you must make a difficult choice: enter recovery or get worse.

Entering recovery is not easy. It means having to admit things about yourself that are embarrassing and ugly. It means that someone else will have to hear your story of brokenness, selfishness, foolish decisions, and lack of self-control. You will have to decide if the pain of recovery is worth more than the continued, worsening pain of addiction.

You might lose your reputation if you choose recovery, because now the truth is out. You might lose your spouse. You might lose your children, your job, your possessions, even your life. Although you might lose such things if you choose recovery, it is more likely that you would lose those things *anyway* if you continue down the path of addiction. Any losses in recovery cannot compare with what is ultimately gained: freedom, peace, and joy.

But you might be wondering, *How can grace cause all this change?* I realize that the idea of grace doesn't seem to fit with our normal understanding (or experience) with recovery. We think of recovery in terms of delivering brutal confessions, agonizing amend-making, setting up stringent

---

3. This book is not intended to attack any particular method of recovery, but rather to expose possible fallacies of underlying performance-based principles that are counter to grace-based recovery.

boundaries, keeping high levels of accountability, and working our butts off. And while all those things are very much a part of the recovery process, apart from grace they simply become an idolatrous task list that exhausts the body and soul almost as much as addiction.

Grace changes everything because grace gives you a new lens through which to see the whole process of recovery. Grace reminds you over and over again that your value before God is unchanging regardless of your bad (or good) performance. Grace invites you to an ongoing process of growth in the context of love, joy, and authentic community.

Here are some possible differences between a grace-based perspective and a performance-based perspective and how they might affect recovery.

Grace-Based Recovery	Performance-Based Recovery
Personal value is a constant.	Personal value fluctuates, based on behavior.
Confession explores mistakes to learn and grow from them.	Confession punishes bad behavior by a "start over" mentality.
Accountability is an opportunity to build others up in truth and love.	Accountability is a tool to control or force behavioral outcomes.
Allows for safe exploration of wounds, shame, false beliefs, etc.	Focuses on behavior over and above the emotional.
Grace leads to humility.	Performance leads to pride.
Grace shifts focus to God and others.	Performance focuses on me.
Grace sets people free.	Performance manages sin.

I know that this chart can be troubling for some, especially those who have had experiences in highly behaviorally focused programs. My intent is not to upset. I know that many have found help and significant breakthroughs in such settings. But there is no denying the differences between a recovery setting that is primarily focused on behavior modification (performance-based) and one that is focused on the freedom that God desires to give (grace-based)—even if those differences don't play out exactly the way the chart describes.

I have worked with hundreds of addicted individuals over the years and all who have come from performance-based environments have expressed the same sentiment: even after eliminating their addictive behaviors, something was still missing. They still felt "unfree" from something. In other words, simply "not acting out" was not real freedom, not true recovery. This is where grace must enter the journey. Without the favor and kindness of God, there is no freedom, even if you never act out again.

Spend some time asking God to show you his grace. Open yourself up to this wonderful gift. Read and reread Titus 2:11-14 and ask God to show you how he wants to manifest his grace in your life and recovery. Don't rush this conversation. Sit in grace and let it soak to your bones. Be enveloped by the truth that in Jesus Christ, your value to God is unchangeable—he really does love you! When that truth sinks deep into your soul, you will know the grace of God—and it will change everything.

DISCUSSION QUESTIONS

1. Define "grace." Why is God's grace so important to your personal recovery?
2. Thinking about all that you could lose as a result of your addiction, share your top reasons for why you are committed to recovery. Now ask yourself if those reasons are grounded in your relationship with God or in your own ability and strength. How can you move more toward a grace motivation (following God's instruction and lead) rather than a performance motivation (following your own wisdom and ideas)?
3. Why is a grace-based recovery approach actually hard to practice? What is required in order to truly receive (embrace) grace? (Hint: Think of the differences between humility and pride.)
4. Review the chart of differences between Grace-Based and Performance-Based recovery. Where in your own recovery have you seen more of a performance-based approach rather than grace-based? How can you take more of a grace-based approach moving forward?

GROUP EXERCISE

Celebrate God!

In grace-based recovery, all celebrations of victory give the credit to God rather than yourself. Why? Because recovery is a *gift* of God's grace. Therefore, he deserves the glory, not you. This kind of celebrating can be difficult to do, when it feels very much like you were the one who resisted the temptation to act out! But remember, it is *grace* that trains us "to renounce ungodliness and worldly passions." Even victories are a gift of God's grace.

Go around the group and share a victory from the past week. Keeping in mind that victories are gifts from God, share how this changes your perspective and attitude toward the specific victory you shared. Spend time together celebrating God for giving you all you needed to resist temptation and "live self-controlled, upright, and godly" in that moment.

2

Grace to Share Your Story

Main idea: Tell your story, tell the truth

Bible passage: 1 John 1:5-10

GBR article: Telling the truth about yourself

Discussion questions

Group exercise: How to tell the truth (the truth, the whole truth, nothing but the truth)

MAIN IDEA

The effect of God's grace is only fully realized when you bring your unfiltered story of brokenness into the light. You cannot keep your story hidden and expect to be transformed into a new person who is free from strongholds. Your *full* story must be told. It is the key step to "walking in the light" and beginning the healing journey of recovery.

BIBLE PASSAGE

1 John 1:5-10

This is the message we have heard from him and proclaim to you, that God is light, and in him is no darkness at all. If we say we have fellowship with him while we walk in darkness, we lie and do not practice the truth. But if we walk in the light, as he is in the light, we have fellowship with one another, and the blood of Jesus his Son cleanses us from all sin. If we say we have no sin, we deceive ourselves, and the truth is not in us. If we confess our sins, he is faithful and just to forgive us our sins and to cleanse us from all unrighteousness. If we say we have not sinned, we make him a liar, and his word is not in us.

ARTICLE

2

Telling the Truth about Yourself

You can never break free from addiction without telling the truth—the whole truth! God's grace covers your sin but never excuses it. To lie in recovery is to turn 180 degrees and walk right back into the darkness you want to flee. Addiction is a house of lies and the only way to tear down lies is with the truth. Therefore, you must tell someone your story of brokenness.

Grace-based recovery invites you to tell your full story, because there is nothing that you could reveal that God does not already know. Honesty is about building your character and learning how to "walk in the light," no longer willing to carry around secrets that slowly snuff out your life.

I must admit that this is a difficult challenge. Addicts are pros when it comes to lying; it is how the addiction stays hidden and perpetuates. This is why it is so difficult to come out of the dark and tell your full story. To be known is a risk.

I remember vividly the first time I was encouraged by my counselor to step into a support group and share my story. It was only a few weeks after I began meeting with this counselor. I felt terror. I had shared my story with the counselor but it felt safe because he was bound by law not to retell my story to anyone else. But now I was being invited to share with people who didn't come with that same kind of legal protection. I was scared. But I did it. And I'm glad I did. My life has never been the same since.

By definition, "walking in the light" will expose whatever you have been carrying in the dark. And because what you have been carrying in the dark is exactly what you have been trying to hide, it will be painful to bring it into the light. But if you never tell your full story, you will never experience full freedom.

Grace-based recovery gives you the courage to do difficult things so that you might discover God's best for your life.

GRACE-BASED RECOVERY ACCEPTS YOUR STORY OF BROKENNESS

Oftentimes, recovery programs become so focused on moving an addict forward to places of cleaned-up behavior and radical lifestyle changes that they fail to embrace or accept the brokenness of the person in front of them. Grace embraces you, *all* of you.

Sometimes this level of acceptance is hard to receive. You have probably beaten yourself up so much and immersed yourself in shame for so long that to have someone invite you to tell your story and not shun you as a result might feel shocking. But it is necessary to let others into your story, into the broken places where you have been wounded, lied to, and calloused. It is okay to feel awkward in the presence of grace, but I assure you that, over time, it will become your favorite place to be. It is the place where community, love, and godly character exist and grow.

Many people assume that grace would be easy to receive. But so few have experienced real grace-filled environments, they don't actually have a clue as to whether it would be easy or not. Then, when they do enter a grace-based environment, they are hit with the shock that it wasn't as easy as they assumed to receive the free gift of complete, unmerited acceptance.

If it takes you a while to warm up to the idea that others (even God) could receive you this way, be patient with yourself. Everybody who enters into grace-based recovery squirms at first. Many spend a lot of energy trying to prove themselves worthy, pointing out all the good things they have started to do in recovery in an attempt to feel like they did something to earn the gift of grace. But that is not how grace works. It is free!

God knew your story—all of it—before you were born. All your sin. All your failures. All your shame. And yet he chose to make a way for you to be connected to him forever through the life, death, and resurrection of Jesus Christ. When you trust in Christ for the forgiveness of your sins, you are given eternal life with God. May this glorious gift of grace from God give you the confidence to tell your story to someone else!

GRACE-BASED RECOVERY ALWAYS LEAVES THE DOOR OPEN

You will not "walk in the light" perfectly. You will stumble on this journey of recovery. So how does a grace-based group respond when the unfolding of each member's story is rough and imperfect?

There is no "three-strikes-and-you're-out" in grace-based recovery. Grace always welcomes home the stray addict. Always! If we truly want to see lives changed and addicts set free, we can never close the door on one another, no matter how often or for how long we might fall. Grace cannot be measured. (After all, how can you quantify something that is free?) Grace can only be poured out.

In Luke 15 there is a great story about a son who is selfish and arrogant. He squanders his father's wealth in a foreign country and eventually finds himself starving to death in a pig pen. Finally, broken and exhausted over his sin, he returns to his father to see if he can just be one of the servants in his house. But his dad sees him coming down the road and sprints to embrace him, kiss him, and throw a party for his return. This boy was not rejected when he came crawling home. He was met with grace from a loving father. This is what grace-based recovery must look like for the wayward addict.

When an addict falls in recovery (notice I said *when*) and repents, he must be allowed back into the group. If he is left outside, it will only reinforce a performance-based recovery that strictly sees a person's value to the group in terms of his behavior. But grace sees the addict's value regardless of behavior. And besides, it is *inside* the group where the returning addict will get the help needed to keep moving toward recovery, healing, and wholeness.

Is grace-based recovery what you want? Then jump in. Tell your full story, and keep telling your story as it unfolds in the light of God's faithful grace. And never forget that God is keenly interested in your story—all of it!

DISCUSSION QUESTIONS

1. What scares you the most about being fully known? How do you typically respond to such fears?
2. Respond to this statement: "If you never tell your full story, you will never experience full freedom." Why is this true?
3. Is "telling your story" a one-time event? Why is it important to continue telling your story throughout your recovery and growth?
4. What are some positive effects of telling your full story to safe people? *(Suggested answers: it fosters humility, exposes areas that need work, invites friendship, etc.)*
5. How can you overcome the shame that fights against you telling your full story?

2

GROUP EXERCISE

How to Tell the Truth

Telling your story is an exercise in telling the truth about yourself. But addiction teaches you the opposite: how to lie about (and to) yourself. This means that a huge part of recovery is simply learning how to tell the truth. I know it sounds ridiculous, but when you have been so conditioned by addict-thinking, it can be more difficult than you realize to simply speak truthfully—about anything!

A simple way to begin speaking more truthfully is to ask yourself these three questions before opening your mouth:

1. Is it true? In other words, is it factual?
2. Is it the whole truth? Are you trying to leave anything out or are you declaring the full reality?
3. Is it nothing but the truth? Are you embellishing or adding to the facts?

As your group exercise, do the following. Think of one thing that happened in your life in the last twenty-four to forty-eight hours. It can be anything; it doesn't have to be related to recovery. Share what happened and how it made you feel, filtering the occurrence through the three questions above (Truth, Whole Truth, Nothing but the Truth). Then discuss with one another how you think this exercise will help you become a more truthful person.

3

Grace to Belong

Main idea: Authentic community, healing wounds

Bible passages: Ecclesiastes 4:9-12; John 15:12-17

GBR article: Where healing and growth happen

Discussion questions

Group exercise: Making friends (more than one-dimensional)

MAIN IDEA

Addiction leads to loneliness. It has a way of driving people out of your life because addiction is so self-focused. There is little room for empathy or care for others in addiction. Therefore, recovery is a process of learning how to live and thrive in community—real community, not merely being around people. You need people who know and love you. You also need people you can know and love. You need a place to belong. And grace-based recovery creates such environments.

BIBLE PASSAGES

Ecclesiastes 4:9-12

Two are better than one, because they have a good reward for
their toil. For if they fall, one will lift up his fellow. But woe to
him who is alone when he falls and has not another to lift him
up! Again, if two lie together, they keep warm, but how can one
keep warm alone? And though a man might prevail against one
who is alone, two will withstand him—a threefold cord is not
quickly broken.

John 15:12-17

"This is my commandment, that you love one another as I have
loved you. Greater love has no one than this, that someone lay
down his life for his friends. You are my friends if you do what I
command you. No longer do I call you servants, for the servant
does not know what his master is doing; but I have called you
friends, for all that I have heard from my Father I have made
known to you. You did not choose me, but I chose you and
appointed you that you should go and bear fruit and that your
fruit should abide, so that whatever you ask the Father in my
name, he may give it to you. These things I command you, so
that you will love one another."

Lesson

3

ARTICLE

Where Healing and Growth Happen

Most addicts believe recovery is for the sole purpose of correcting out-of-control compulsions. If you are a drug addict or an alcoholic, recovery will help you stop drinking or doing drugs. If you are a sex or food addict, recovery will help you stop acting out sexually or overeating. This is the "healing" most addicts seek in recovery. But that is not what needs healing.

Jesus spent a lot of time in his ministry correcting religious leaders for their misunderstanding and distortion of God's instructions. They tended to look at God's law and interpret it strictly on a behavioral level; what does it tell us to do (or not do)? Jesus even suggested that they flawlessly performed the letter of the law (Matthew 5:20), while they grossly missed the heart of it.

> He [Jesus] went on from there and entered their synagogue. And a man was there with a withered hand. And they asked him, "Is it lawful to heal on the Sabbath?"—so that they might accuse him. He said to them, "Which one of you who has a sheep, if it falls into a pit on the Sabbath, will not take hold of it and lift it out? Of how much more value is a man than a sheep! So it is lawful to do good on the Sabbath." Then he said to the man, "Stretch out your hand." And the man stretched it out, and it was restored, healthy like the other. But the Pharisees went out and conspired against him, how to destroy him. (Matthew 12:9-14)

These Pharisees knew the letter of the law—that one shouldn't "work" on the Sabbath— but they totally missed the heart of it. Jesus exposed these men for their hypocrisy and lack of compassion. Their rigid adherence to the rules created hard hearts that sought more to control others than to care for them. Jesus, on the other hand, showed them the heart of the law, that "it is lawful to do good on the Sabbath."

When Jesus healed that guy's hand, do you think the healed man cared what day of the week it was? Neither did Jesus. At the heart of God's law is love. Jesus didn't break the law by healing this man; he embodied the law, the law of love.

If you are addicted to something, you have a history of being wounded. Some of your wounds may be physical, other wounds are emotional or verbal, possibly even spiritual. These wounds often become a foundational element of what eventually led you toward addiction. There is no such thing as an unscarred addict.

The wounds in your soul need healing. When you share your full story, these wounds will come to the surface, and the pain you feel today may be just as powerful as when you were first hurt. But Jesus can carry you through the pain to a place of healing and restoration in your soul. You do not have to continue living under the weight of unhealed wounds.

God's grace helps you heal by reminding you that you are worth saving; you are worth your recovery. Some may say that because of what you have done, you aren't worth saving. You should rot in hell or at least be made to suffer for what you have done. But God sees beyond your acting out and looks at the wounded soul inside, the little child who was neglected, beaten, raped, left to fend for himself, or was never good enough. God sees your brokenness and offers you a pathway to healing.

It takes time to heal from deep wounds in your soul. You must be patient with yourself. You must examine areas of your heart that have probably been hidden for a long time. You need grace, not law, to encourage you to keep going when you grow weary and want to give up. Grace offers you time, however long it takes to heal.

COMMUNITY IS WHERE HEALING THRIVES

It is one thing to know that your wounds need healing. It is another thing entirely to actually begin the healing process. While this study will not address all the facets of that process, it is important that we direct you to the environment where the healing effects of grace thrive: Christ-centered, Christ-empowered community.

The entire point of this grace-based recovery study is that we need safe, grace-filled environments to unpack our brokenness and pursue God's best for our lives. Essential to this process is community—the fellowship, encouragement, and accountability of other Christ-followers, who know what it is to be known, forgiven, and made new by Jesus. You will never experience the fullness of healing (physical, emotional, and spiritual) in isolation. God designed you to belong—to him and to other Christ-followers. We need each other if we are to heal and grow in our recovery.

When I think about the importance of community to healing in recovery, the image that comes to mind is that of a hospital. If you broke your leg, you would not assume that such an injury could heal without the involvement of others. You would need someone to transport you to professional help. You would need a doctor or surgeon to assess the damage and prescribe the right treatment. You would need nurses, pharmacists, physical therapists, and more to walk you through (no pun intended) all the stages in the healing of your broken leg. In addition, you would need the emotional support of friends and family and the spiritual support of the Holy Spirit and your church family. You would need community to heal from a broken leg.

So ask yourself this question: how much *more* do you think you need a Christ-centered community to heal from the wounds connected to your addictive strongholds?

Christ-centered community is a nonnegotiable necessity for true recovery to happen.

DISCUSSION QUESTIONS

1. How would you define authentic community? What makes such a community different from a crowd of acquaintances?
2. Do you know what wounds need healing in your life (emotional, physical, spiritual)? If not, are you willing to seek help to uncover them?
3. Why is community essential to healing and growth in recovery? What has been your experience in trying to heal and grow apart from community?
4. What does it feel like to belong? To be "known and loved" by someone? What can be scary about this?
5. What makes someone a true friend? How would you define "faithful friendship"?

Lesson

GROUP EXERCISE

Making Friends

To recover from addiction, you need friends—faithful friends! A recovery community is a great environment to establish and build such friendships. But what makes these friendships effective? A good friend in recovery will

- listen.
- hold you accountable to your boundaries.
- encourage you when you stumble and help you learn from it.
- point you to God's truth and love.
- share their life with you.
- pray *for* you and *with* you.

Faithful friendship is not merely about recovery. It is about a bond that is mutually beneficial for growing in God's grace and truth. Be careful not to make "friends" that are one-dimensional, only focused on recovery and accountability.

As a group, discuss how you might pursue "faithful friendships" together. This doesn't mean you must "force" friendships with each other. The question is, rather, how can you help each other pursue such friendships, even if they are with others outside the group?

Lesson

4

Grace to Get Back Up

Main idea: Dealing with failure in recovery

Bible passage: James 5:13-16

GBR article: How grace teaches us to learn from failure

Discussion questions

Group exercise: Practicing true confession

MAIN IDEA

Recovery is an imperfect journey of stumbling in the right direction. No one travels the road of recovery without falling. No one! This doesn't mean that you are aiming for failure, simply that it is inevitable. But God is more than able to pick you up and give you what you need to take another step. Remember, his grace reminds you that your worth to him is not based on your perfection, but rather on his love.

Jesus is the only one to ever live a perfectly sinless life before God. And because God loves you, the sinless Jesus took the punishment for your sins, dying on your behalf so that your sins might be forgiven. Despite your sinfulness, God considered you worth the life of his perfect Son.

Knowing that God loves you this way, your response to your failures in recovery should lead you to confess them to God, which is followed by repentance. Don't be deceived into thinking that confession was a one-time necessity at the beginning of recovery that never needs to be repeated, or that what you learned in your first step of recovery was all you would ever need to know.

Confession and repentance are core disciplines of recovery. When you stumble, you must confess that to God and to some faithful friends. You must repent of false beliefs about your identity and value to God and any wrong steps you have taken. When you confess and repent, you break the power of darkness, and Jesus, the Light of hope and healing, lifts you up to keep moving forward.

BIBLE PASSAGE

James 5:13-16

Is anyone among you suffering? Let him pray. Is anyone cheerful? Let him sing praise. Is anyone among you sick? Let him call for the elders of the church, and let them pray over him, anointing him with oil in the name of the Lord. And the prayer of faith will save the one who is sick, and the Lord will raise him up. And if he has committed sins, he will be forgiven. Therefore, confess your sins to one another and pray for one another, that you may be healed. The prayer of a righteous person has great power as it is working.

Lesson

4

ARTICLE

How Grace Teaches Us to Learn from Failure

Failure is inevitable on the pathway to success. This may seem at first like a falsehood. But give yourself a moment to think about it. Name one person who reached any pinnacle of success without being affected by failure. Everyone in life faces failures, mistakes, and detours, whether by their own choices or the choices of others. The universal reality of all mankind is summed up in Romans 3:23, "For all have sinned and fall short of the glory of God."

So how does failure tie to success? Every failure is an opportunity to learn. Thomas Edison, when asked about his many failed attempts at inventing the light bulb, is quoted as saying, "I have not failed. I've just found ten thousand ways that won't work." If failure is viewed as a stop sign, you will cease pursuing "ways that work." But if failure is seen as an opportunity to learn and correct course, you will eventually "see the Light" (pun intended).

The trick to turning failure into success is all in how you respond to your stumbles in recovery. You must develop the one-two punch disciplines of confession and repentance. And you must practice these disciplines in a place we have already introduced: community.

Confession: Uncovering what you did in the dark

Confession is agreeing with the truth, or bringing into the light what is hidden in the dark. It sounds so simple, right? And it is, but that doesn't make it easy to do, especially if you have been compiling secret sins for years. But any real recovery must start—and continue—with confessing what is hidden.

Grace helps you to confess, because it promises that whatever you bring out of the dark won't change how God loves you. It is okay if you do not fully believe this right now. Remember, grace is not easy to receive. But it is still true; your secrets and stumbles do not affect your worth. Embracing this can give you the courage you need to open up and confess every time you fall.

Maybe you have already confessed your secrets to God, and that is good. But you might wonder why you are not free from your addiction. It is not because God is powerless or uncaring. It is because you must also confess to fellow believers. Remember the James passage at the beginning of this lesson? "Confess your sins *to one another* and pray for one another, that you may be healed" (5:16, emphasis mine).

This passage teaches that your sins are not only to be confessed to God (as in 1 John 1:9), but they must also be confessed to one another. Why? So you might be healed, no longer bound by the darkness of secrecy, lies, and shame. You must bring what is hidden out into the open to learn from it, and grace can help you do that.

When you confess, take time to unpack all the steps that led up to the sin and all your reactions afterward. These are clues into your heart. The stumbles in recovery are never only about behavior; they are about motives, thoughts, passions, and wounds. If you simply confess to the behavior without exploring all that surrounded it, you will do little to correct your course the next time you are faced with similar temptations

This is why it is critical to confess "to one another" and allow trusted friends to help you with your blind spots. Together, and by God's leading, you can discover the areas that need the most attention for making the next best steps forward.

Repentance: Aligning your thoughts and motives with truth

Confession in recovery is only the first step in responding properly to failures. This must be followed up with repentance. To repent is to "change your mind" in the right direction. It is like confession in the sense that you admit to wrong thinking, but it goes further than confession by engaging your will to do something about it. Confession reveals your error and repentance corrects it.

To repent well, it is essential that God's Word, the Bible, be your ultimate source for truth and wisdom. Friends are good. Counselors are helpful. Even pastors have their strategic place in your recovery. But none are a substitute for the eternal, inerrant Word of God. You must discipline yourself to "change your mind" toward the truth of Scripture. This is the true discipline of repentance.

Grace-based recovery is a journey of ever-growing success. If you want to enjoy such success, you must confess and repent when you stumble. Here is the basic progression of this confession-repentance process:

1. You stumble in some way.
2. You confess what you did to God and trusted friends.
3. You unpack the details surrounding the stumble to uncover false beliefs, wrong motives, and other errors in thinking or decision-making.
4. You repent of any untruths in thinking and replace them with the truths of God's Word.
5. You construct a plan with trusted friends for a better response to similar temptations down the road.
6. You pray and keep pressing on.

Though failure is inevitable along the road of recovery, it doesn't need to define the outcome of your journey. Devote yourself to confession and repentance so that you can learn from your mistakes and enjoy the long-term success of a grace-based recovery.

DISCUSSION QUESTIONS

1. What is the difference between confession and repentance? How do these differences complement each other?
2. Why are both confession and repentance necessary when responding to failure in recovery? Why couldn't you simply respond with confession *or* repentance?
3. James 5:16 instructs us to "pray for one another" in addition to confessing our sins to one another. Why is this additional instruction important? What do you think such prayer looks like?
4. Why is it important to unpack what happened before and after your sinful behavior and not just the behavior itself?
5. How can you better adopt a mindset of learning from your mistakes?

Lesson

4

GROUP EXERCISE

Practicing True Confession

Let's not pretend that confession and repentance are easy disciplines to practice. But you wouldn't have gotten this far in this study if you hadn't already done some hard things in recovery. Admitting you need help is a hard thing to do, and here you are. So, just because something is hard to do doesn't mean that it isn't the right thing to do. Much of recovery is learning to do hard things that are good for you. Confessing when you mess up is good to do. Repenting and turning your mind toward truth is good to do.

As a group, let's practice true confession and repentance. And remember, this is a No Shame Zone, so everyone is here to help and support each other toward success!

Everyone, think of one instance of failure in your past that you can confess (even if it has been confessed before; this is about practice). But rather than just confess the behavior, think about the factors that led up to it and the reactions you had afterward. Make this part of the confession too.

- What triggered you?
- Where did your thoughts go?
- What emotions did you feel?
- Can you connect those emotions to anything in your past? Your childhood?
- What did you feel afterward?
- What did you think afterward?
- What did you do afterward?

As you confess these experiences, take note of any lies, false beliefs, wounds, misdirected motives, etc. that come out. These are the points at which repentance will be necessary, and the points where correction for future encounters can be made.

Spend time praying for each other and encouraging each other toward greater honesty and openness.

5

Grace to Persevere

Main idea: Embracing faithfulness

Bible passage: James 1:22-25; Proverbs 27:17

GBR article: Keep on keeping on

Discussion questions

Group exercise: Daily disciplines that affect freedom

MAIN IDEA

Grace-based recovery is not a short journey. Recovery is a process and the process takes time—but not *just* time. Recovery is an active process of embarking on entirely new ways to think, relate, and act. This requires faithful endurance on your part to stick with this process through all its peaks and valleys. You must learn to persevere if you expect to be set free from addictive strongholds.

BIBLE PASSAGE

James 1:22-25

But be doers of the word, and not hearers only, deceiving your-
selves. For if anyone is a hearer of the word and not a doer, he is
like a man who looks intently at his natural face in a mirror. For
he looks at himself and goes away and at once forgets what he
was like. But the one who looks into the perfect law, the law of
liberty, and perseveres, being no hearer who forgets but a doer
who acts, he will be blessed in his doing.

Proverbs 27:17

Iron sharpens iron,
    and one man sharpens another.

5

ARTICLE

Keep on Keeping On

Most recovery programs, as we've stated in earlier lessons, focus solely (or at least primarily) on modifying or controlling behavior. But that is not what recovery really needs to be about. That is a shallow and short-term vision. Grace-based recovery calls you to be faithful in recovery, in relationships, in life.

Faithfulness is about remaining true to a person, a cause, or a belief. This is a tall order for an addict, because addiction simply follows wherever the urges might lead. There is no loyalty or fidelity in addiction. If a "better offer" comes along, the addicted person lunges toward it without any thought of the consequences.

Recovery is good because it leads to sanity and sobriety. It helps you step off the "merry-go-round" of craziness that only spins faster and faster the longer you ride it. In recovery you are finally able to stop long enough to clear your head, find your bearings, and focus on a pathway to real change and health.

It is incredibly important that you learn to be faithful in the process of recovery. This requires saying no to urges you have always allowed, committing to healthy outlets for dealing with temptation, and keeping your word. To be faithful is to embrace recovery and be loyal to the process, especially when you are tempted to step off the path.

However, when you do step off the path, as someone who is growing in faithfulness, you will more quickly return to your recovery. By grace, your stumbling can never disqualify you from the journey. Faithfulness is not about never failing, but rather about always eventually returning to your commitment to recovery when you do fall.

FAITHFULNESS: DOING THE RIGHT THING OVER AND OVER AGAIN

God's Word reminds us that it isn't enough to just know the truth. God expects us to "do" the truth. To put this in recovery language, it isn't enough to just know what freedom and sobriety are; you must do what free and sober people do. Grace-based recovery means becoming acquainted experientially with your true identity in Christ as a free, faithful child of God. This isn't a process of just gaining more head knowledge. It's time to put what you already know into practice.

I would be shocked if you told me that you didn't know the right thing to do in relationship to your particular addictive struggle. In other words, your problem is not ignorance. You know the difference between right and wrong, between sober and addicted. You know where that line is because you have crossed it many times. So don't pretend that your struggle is with knowledge. It isn't! Your struggle is with practice. You struggle with applying your will, by God's grace, to do the right thing. (It's okay; this is the basic struggle for every human being!)

I'm not saying that you can't grow in your knowledge of what is right. We can all benefit from a deeper knowledge of truth. But there are limits to knowledge. And the kind of "knowing" that an addict needs is rarely intellectual. An addict needs to know the truth the way a carpenter knows his hammer. A carpenter doesn't carry around a picture of a hammer, pull it out at his jobsite, and explain how it works to the customer. No, he carries an *actual* hammer and "knows" it by repeatedly swinging it to complete the job. He may not hit the nail every time, but he has swung it enough to know how it operates in action, not just in theory.

You, too, will need to pick up the "hammer" of recovery and get to swinging it. I know you won't hit the nail every time (maybe for a long time), but it's the only way you can "do" recovery. This hammer of recovery contains all the basic principles of a life of integrity (confession, repentance, self-awareness, faith, community, service). As you grow in your faithful practice of grace-based recovery, your skill in each area will improve. Not because you know *about* such principles, but rather because you are *practicing* such principles in your daily life. You must swing the hammer every day.

PERSISTENCE WILL PAY OFF— EVENTUALLY

Grace-based recovery leads you on a *long* journey, not because recovery is about seeing how much you can suffer, but because real transformation takes a long time. No one gets well overnight. This means that persistence is key to long-term change.

Proverbs 27:17 (one of this lesson's Bible passages) is often used as the theme verse for men's ministries. It paints a great picture of iron being sharpened into useful tools or weapons. But the poetic nature of the verse may cause one to miss the grueling reality it portrays.

Imagine that you held two iron rods in your hands. Each is eighteen inches long and rounded. You need to put a sharp edge on both rods but can only use the other rod to do so. What does this picture look like now? Poetic? Fast? Easy?

You will actually have quite a long process ahead of you. You must press the rods into each other—hard! This will create pressure, heat, friction, and even sparks when the imperfections in each rod strike against the other. All of sudden you realize that this is no easy, fast process. In order to create sharp rods, you must be persistent.

The same is true of becoming a "sharp" man or woman of sobriety, no longer bound to your addictive ways. You must press into others on the journey, expecting friction, pressure, and sparks that fly. But you must not give up on the process! If at any point you stop pressing in, you both will suffer.

If you chose to stop striking those iron rods against each other, what likelihood is there that a sharp edge would appear on either rod? None! You must continue applying pressure in order to sharpen the rods. You must also continue pressing into other "rods" (people) in your recovery if you (and they) are to become sharp and useful.

Grace allows us the time we need to persist in recovery. Pressure, friction, heat, and sparks are very unpleasant on the journey, even if we know what the intended result is meant to be. When you grow weary and decide to coast, grace reminds you of your value, and the value of those on the journey with you. It invites you to keep pressing in even though you are tired.

Giving up only results in your addiction getting worse. Keep pressing on in recovery and you will become a powerful weapon for good, not only in your life but in the lives of those around you.

DISCUSSION QUESTIONS

1. What makes quitting recovery seem so attractive at times? How can you better resist such temptations?
2. In what areas do you struggle most in being faithful? What is one thing you could do this week to improve in those areas?
3. How can you better apply your knowledge of recovery to your daily practices to combat temptation and grow in grace and truth?
4. Why does "giving up only result in getting worse"?
5. In what areas of your recovery are you not "swinging the hammer"? What will you do this week to sharpen your focus and persist in "doing" recovery?

5

GROUP EXERCISE

Daily Disciplines That Affect Freedom

This lesson's article lists six principles that make up the "hammer" of recovery you are to "work out" daily: confession, repentance, self-awareness, faith, community, service. This group exercise will help you start outlining specific actions you can take to grow your skill in these areas.

Take a piece of paper or a journal and write down the six principles listed. For each principle, share something specific that you could do to grow in that area. For example, for "faith" you could

- read your Bible every day before going to work.
- pray (alone, with your spouse, with a friend, at a prayer meeting, etc.).
- attend a Bible study in your church or community.
- regularly attend worship at a local church.

Share your ideas with each other and encourage accountability for pursuing at least one specific area in the coming week. Be careful not to add too many things to your list. Pursue faithfulness in a few specific disciplines and increase your commitments gradually. It is through faithfulness and perseverance that one grows "sharp" in God's kingdom.

6

Grace to Forgive

Main idea: The two sides of forgiveness

Bible passage: Colossians 3:12-13

GBR article: The grace to make amends

Discussion questions

Group exercise: Living out the Golden Rule

MAIN IDEA

Sin hurts people. I could have said "addiction hurts people" and that would have been true too. But the engine of addiction is sin. It is a disease that has infected every human being since Adam and Eve. And sin hurts people. It hurts the offended as well as the offender. Sin causes wounds. And wounds need healing if true recovery is going to happen.

The cure for sin's wounds is not psychology, or psychiatry, or sincere promises. The cure is forgiveness, but not the world's kind of forgiveness that comes with all kinds of strings attached. The forgiveness that heals sin's wounds can only originate from God. This is why grace-based recovery is so important. Apart from the forgiveness we are given by God, there is no hope for real freedom or change or life. This is the forgiveness you must receive if you want real transformation.

BIBLE PASSAGE

Colossians 3:12-13

Put on then, as God's chosen ones, holy and beloved, compassionate hearts, kindness, humility, meekness, and patience, bearing with one another and, if one has a complaint against another, forgiving each other; as the Lord has forgiven you, so you also must forgive.

6

The Grace to Make Amends

Every addict has been hurt by someone else, and every addict has also hurt someone they love. Since addicts learn to cope with pain through abusive means (drugs, alcohol, cutting, porn, illicit sex, etc.), they tend to transmit the pain they suffered onto others. Therefore, if real change is going to occur, forgiveness is essential.

Remember Joe? Let's check back with him now.

"Joe, so good to see you back at group this week. And thanks for sharing about some of your really tough childhood. I'm so sorry your neighbor took advantage of you like that. That must have been really painful and confusing."

"It was. For years I felt such debilitating shame about the whole thing. I felt like I was to blame, but I also didn't know what I could have done about it. I mean, he was six years older than I was and I never felt like I had a choice. Over time, I hated myself as much as I hated him. I still hate him. I know I'm supposed to forgive him for what he did, but I don't know how to let go of my anger and hate."

"What if I told you that you didn't need to let go of it right now? How would that make you feel?"

"Good, I guess. But at the same time I can't stand carrying around all this hatred. I'm just such an angry person and I seem to be able to trace it all back to him. I mean, I like the idea of not putting so much pressure on myself to forgive, but I'm tired of carrying the hate."

"Why don't we work on your heart first? Then we can deal with thinking about forgiving your neighbor. You might find that forgiveness will seem more palatable when you start gaining a new view of yourself. When you begin to see yourself as God sees you, through the lens of love, you might feel more of a freedom to offer your neighbor the forgiveness he doesn't deserve."

"That's a relief. It seems like every Christian I've talked to has just added to the pressure I already feel to forgive that jerk, but I just don't want to. I would like to do what you're saying and see if I could start to see myself differently. Because right now I can only see myself as a damaged scumbag."

Forgiveness is a process, a painful and difficult one. There is agony in forgiveness because it requires forgivers to choose *not* to punish the one who offended them. Joe's neighbor deserved to be punished for what he did—severely! That's why Joe's process of forgiveness wasn't easy. He had to decide if he wanted to release his neighbor from the penalty he deserved. That is no easy decision.

Too often in recovery, well-meaning people give bad advice regarding forgiveness. Some handle it too lightly and make it an optional part of recovery. But a failure to forgive always results in further bondage to one's abuser. Others handle forgiveness too rigidly, demanding that this tough decision be made immediately, without regard for the addict's deep wounds. Neither way is helpful.

Grace offers another avenue for forgiveness, a way that takes into account the pain suffered and the need for a new perspective on it, a new vantage point. Most addicts have been reeling from the pain of their wounds for years, building up decades of resentment and hatred toward their abusers.

Over time, addicts develop intense shame and then, as a result of their own addiction, they end up hurting others. This means that their vantage point is that of a bitter, angry victim. On some level, they probably feel like they deserve exactly what their abusers deserve. And in one respect (as sinful human beings who have rebelled against their Creator) they are right. But this blinds addicts from seeing clearly what their wounds were all about: someone else's brokenness got dumped into their life.

Joe wasn't to blame for what his neighbor did to him, even if Joe later went along with it. That was his neighbor's brokenness, not Joe's. But twenty-five years later, when Joe was ready to work on recovery from his own addiction, he couldn't see the abuse so clearly. He blamed himself, hated himself, and cursed himself, all for what his neighbor did to him.

Grace pulls back the curtain that hides the little kid inside you. It shows you that what happened to that kid was not your fault. It wasn't right or good, but it wasn't your fault. This allows you to begin healing from the wounds, so that you can eventually take the next step toward forgiveness.

It is likely that when you start seeing how someone else's brokenness was forced into your life, you will become even angrier. Not necessarily a vengeful kind of anger, but more like a righteous anger. You may weep over your child self who was unable to fight off the abuser. You may feel deep pain that in some ways hurts even more than the original abuse did. This is normal. Yet this can be healing when you release this pain to God and entrust justice to his timetable and methods.

When you gain this new view of your past wounds and have felt a cleansing of your soul through grieving your losses,[1] you will be in a much better place to work on forgiveness. Grieving alone cannot fully release you from your past; you must forgive. This is where grace comes in.

> Put on then, as God's chosen ones, holy and beloved, compassionate hearts, kindness, humility, meekness, and patience,

---

1. Professional counseling can be helpful when dealing with past abuse and wounds. For help finding a counselor, visit AACC.net or call 1-800-A-FAMILY.

bearing with one another and, if one has a complaint against another, forgiving each other; **as the Lord has forgiven you, so you also must forgive**. (Colossians 3:12-13, emphasis mine)

The best way to understand how to forgive someone who hurt you is to understand how God has forgiven you. You have offended God with your sin (me too; see Romans 6:23). You deserve to be punished for your sins (me too; see Romans 6:23 again). But God instead chooses to forgive (Romans 3:21-24; Ephesians 1:7; Colossians 2:13-15; 1 John 1:9). He chooses the law of love, to pay the price you owed (death) to give you a gift you did not deserve (eternal life). As you meditate on that truth and embrace it deep in your soul, your heart will have the strength, security, and freedom to begin to soften toward those who hurt you.

Keep in mind, though, that forgiveness is a choice. Your feelings may not coincide with what you know you must do. This does not mean that feelings don't matter when it comes to forgiveness; only that they are not the determining factor in choosing to forgive those who have wronged you.

Forgiveness doesn't always mean that there will be a restoration of relationships, nor should it. Some people are unhealthy and dangerous. Forgiveness is simply one of the means by which you will be released from the shackles of anger, fear, and shame that bind you to your past wounds. And God's grace is what will carry you through as you ask him for his help, wisdom and strength to walk this road.

WHAT ABOUT THE OTHER SIDE OF FORGIVENESS?

Recovery will teach you two things about wounds: (1) you have been hurt, and (2) you have hurt others. There is no escaping the truth that your addictive patterns have hurt someone else. While you may not have hurt someone as severely as Joe's neighbor hurt him, your self-centered behaviors have offended someone who loves you. This is a wound that needs healing.

You cannot force someone to forgive you, but you can seek to make amends through humble confession and genuine remorse. And even if they choose to withhold forgiveness from you, God sees your heart and promises to honor those who honor him. Seek a clear conscience and to be at peace with everyone. Recovery is messy, but try to make things as right as you possibly can. God will help you.

DISCUSSION QUESTIONS

1. How does it make you feel to know that forgiveness is essential to the recovery process?
2. Is there anyone in your past that you have not forgiven? Anyone in your present? What will you do to begin unpacking that pain?
3. Who have you hurt by your selfish actions? What will you do to express sorrow and repentance?
4. Spend time journaling about how God has forgiven you. Worship and praise him for his grace and kindness toward you.
5. Is anything blocking you from receiving and embracing the forgiveness of God? The forgiveness of others? How can you begin to remove that blockage so you can experience the fullness of forgiveness?

6

GROUP EXERCISE

Living Out the Golden Rule

Did you know that the Golden Rule is from the Bible? It is. Luke 6:31 says, "And as you wish that others would do to you, do so to them." Why are we bringing this up for a group exercise on the topic of forgiveness? Because the Golden Rule is a great way to get ahead of the whole forgiveness issue. When you treat others with empathy, it is very hard to sin against them. Think of it as preempting the need to ask for forgiveness.

But we do need to address the actual practice of forgiveness. As a group, discuss the following two questions and any roadblocks preventing you from taking action:

- Who do you need to forgive?
- Who do you need to make amends with?

7

Grace to Grow Up

Main idea: Growing in body, soul, and spirit—for a greater purpose

Bible passages: 1 Corinthians 13:11; Ephesians 2:8-10

GBR article: The skill (and art) of growing up

Discussion questions

Group exercise: How to put away childish ways

MAIN IDEA

Addiction breeds immaturity. Don't take this too personally! No one who gets addicted to anything did so exclusively as an adult. In other words, the roots of addiction always form in childhood. Therefore, once any addictive pattern takes hold, it will water those roots of childish thought and reasoning—the idea that life is all about me.

Grace-based recovery, on the other hand, teaches that life is a gift from God. In order to enjoy it properly, you must grow in humility, wisdom, and service. This, essentially, is the exact opposite of childishness. But be warned. Recovery is actually more about what you *pursue* than what you *avoid*. Learn to move toward what is right and you will simultaneously be moving away from what is wrong.

BIBLE PASSAGES

1 Corinthians 13:11

When I was a child, I spoke like a child, I thought like a child, I reasoned like a child. When I became a man, I gave up childish ways.

Ephesians 2:8-10

For by grace you have been saved through faith. And this is not your own doing; it is the gift of God, not a result of works, so that no one may boast. For we are his workmanship, created in Christ Jesus for good works, which God prepared beforehand, that we should walk in them.

7

The Skill (and Art) of Growing Up

Some recovery programs convey an unspoken mandate: you must be "in recovery" for the rest of your life. In other words, if you are not in group or in some other sort of program to manage your addiction, you will not make it. But true recovery is more than simply not acting out. True recovery is about growth in body, soul, and spirit.

Recovery reveals your heart, the good and the bad. You see where you are doing well and you see what needs improvement. There is a lot of self-awareness that comes when you are seriously engaged in recovery.

As these parts of your being are revealed, you start to realize that recovery is about a lot more than your acting-out behaviors. In fact, you start to wonder if this recovery thing is actually about your entire life being transformed. *It is!* From your work to how you talk to managing finances to building relationships to thoughts and motives, recovery is about total transformation.

To say that the vision for your life and future is simply to stop acting out is an incredibly weak vision. How uninspiring! To *not* act out? What kind of a vision is *not* doing something? And what direction would you go next if you succeeded in not acting out? What would you be striving *for* at that point?

Here is a different vision for recovery—a lasting and inspiring vision: to grow in your faith in Christ and service to others. You were made to be whole, fully alive, and thriving in Christ, and to fulfill a purpose that encompasses your mind, body, soul, and spirit. You were not made to continue spiraling downward in a self-destructive pattern of addiction. Do you want to be free? Get on a mission of growth, not merely a mission of "not acting out"!

Grace helps you grow as a person because grace reveals your true identity.

> For by grace you have been saved through faith. And this is not your own doing; it is the gift of God, not a result of works, so that no one may boast. For we are his workmanship, created in Christ Jesus for good works, which God prepared beforehand, that we should walk in them. (Ephesians 2:8-10)

You are the workmanship of God, created for good works. You were made to fulfill a purpose that is God-sized. Recovery that focuses on "not doing" is counter to who you were made to be. You have been given a purpose that is so big that you could not fulfill it, if it were not for God's grace. But because of his grace, you can! Beware, though, of the resistance you will face to this truth.

Shame is often a huge stumbling block to those in recovery. It is behind the lies that cause you to believe you are worthless as a result of your self-ish, addictive actions. It attacks your true identity and calls into question whether anyone (even God) could really love and accept you. It leads you away from who you were made to be. Shame says that you are not worth recovery.

Grace, however, leads you on a different path, one that reminds you that your value is not tied to your failures, and your identity is not based on what you do (or don't do). Grace invites you on a journey of growth, fully aware that you will stumble along the way. But just because you fall, that doesn't mean you cannot get up and press on to uncover the new you.

Embrace a vision of recovery that encompasses your whole being. If you only focus on the spiritual, your emotional and physical self will suffer. If you only focus on your emotional issues, your body and spirit will suffer. If you only focus on the physical (i.e. behavior), your emotional and spiritual selves will languish. You are body, soul, and spirit, so your recovery needs to be about growth in all these areas.

Start with simple things, like your eating and sleeping habits. Make sure you are getting good rest and regular exercise. You don't have to be extreme, but recovery is hard enough without adding to it the trouble that comes from lack of sleep and poor nutrition.

Personal growth is a lifelong venture, not merely a "part" of recovery. Make it your mission to pursue personal growth at every stage of life. You are never too old to keep growing and maturing. And grace allows for all the stumbles that come with such a mission.

No one does recovery perfectly, but for those who commit to growth no matter what it takes, theirs is a new life of incredible fulfillment and joy. And out of such a life come blessings of immeasurable value that can then be poured out on everyone they touch.

FROM CHILD TO ADULT: PUTTING AWAY CHILDISH WAYS

There is a vast difference between child*like* and child*ish*. One leads to faith that can toss mountains into the sea, and the other leaves broken lives and dreams in its wake. God wants to transform your heart to be a giver rather than taker, a lover rather than luster, a servant rather than a master. But he will not force such change on your heart. You must want it.

> When Jesus saw him lying there and knew that he had already been there a long time, he said to him, "Do you want to be healed?" (John 5:6)

In recovery, you will recognize a lot of things about yourself that aren't pretty. You will see that you are broken. You will see that you are selfish. You will see anger, fear, entitlement, pride, and many other characteristics that reveal an adult-sized toddler living deep inside you, who wants his toys and will throw a fit if he doesn't get them. This is the childish you. Grace-based recovery is inviting this "you" to grow up.

Childish you will not be happy during this process. Childish you will whine, scream, stomp around, and demand. But the new you must not give in. The new you must choose to "give up childish ways" in order to grow up to maturity. Be patient with yourself in this process. Extend grace to yourself. Ask God for wisdom and faith to choose what is best and right over what is merely convenient. Commit to growing up and do not allow childish you to reign any longer. The tyranny of childish ways must be ended!

DISCUSSION QUESTIONS

1. In what ways are you still thinking and acting in "childish ways"? How will you "give up" such ways and seek to mature?
2. You were "created in Christ Jesus for good works" (Ephesians 2:10). How does this change your perspective on your recovery journey?
3. Why is "don't act out" a weak vision for recovery?
4. How can you combat the shame and lies that want to keep you stuck in addiction?
5. What are several ways you can focus on growth in body, soul, and spirit in the coming week?

7

How to Put Away Childish Ways

The article in this lesson emphasized the importance of growing in body, soul, and spirit, and giving up childish ways. You might be thinking, *Well, that sounds good, but as one who has lived in such childish ways, how do I recognize my childishness and then give up such ways?* This exercise will help you pursue healthy growth in body, soul, and spirit and, in doing so, begin to expose areas of childish thinking and behaving.

Rank how healthy you believe you are in the following areas (1=weak, 5=strong)

> Physical health
> Emotional health
> Spiritual health
> Relational health

Name one thing you have done in the past week to improve your health in any of these areas.

List as many things as you can that you have done in the past week from pure motives to serve others at your own expense.

List as many things as you can that you have done in the past week from impure motives to serve yourself at someone else's expense.

Discuss these answers with the group and help each other see where your key growth points might be for "giving up childish ways" in favor of more mature, selfless living.

For homework, write down your plan for growth in the areas above and seek accountability from other group members to stick with your plan.

Lesson

8

Grace to Love Well

Main Idea: Love is the goal (grace is to be given away)

Bible passages: John 15:12-14; 1 Peter 4:8

GBR article: The gift worth giving away

Discussion questions

Group exercise: Speaking blessing over others

MAIN IDEA

Grace-based recovery is ultimately about building healthy relationships with God and others. Recovery's primary goal cannot merely be modifying your behavior. The essence of life is not found in behavior; it is found in relationships. Therefore, the goal of true recovery is to love well, not just behave well. Loving God and loving others from a pure heart is the foundation of a life free from the bondage of addiction.

As a result of grace-based recovery, a shift in the focus of your heart from self to others must take place. If you reach the one-year anniversary of your start date of recovery and you still believe that the goal is all about you and your sobriety, you have sadly missed the point. But it's never too late to set your sights on love and to allow the grace and truth of God to transform your heart for the next leg of the journey.

BIBLE PASSAGES

John 15:12-14

"This is my commandment, that you love one another as I have loved you. Greater love has no one than this, that someone lay down his life for his friends. You are my friends if you do what I command you."

1 Peter 4:8

Above all, keep loving one another earnestly, since love covers a multitude of sins.

8

The Gift Worth Giving Away

You were made to be a great lover, not a great luster.

—Stephen Cervantes, HopeCounseling.com

Addiction teaches you to be a taker, someone who does not care about anyone, including yourself. You learn to lie, steal, cheat, abuse, manipulate, and isolate. Life becomes a never-ending pursuit of self-absorbed rituals, all for the momentary pleasure of highs that kill your body, soul, and spirit. But you were made for so much more.

The human heart was made by God to love and be loved. First John 4:9-11 speaks to this truth.

> In this the love of God was made manifest among us, that God sent his only Son into the world, so that we might live through him. In this is love, not that we have loved God but that he loved us and sent his Son to be the propitiation for our sins. Beloved, if God so loved us, we also ought to love one another.

At the core of who you are is a need to be fully known and fully loved. Grace-based recovery reveals your purpose: you were made for love.

Love is fundamentally the opposite of addiction. There is no love in addiction. Love is kind, patient, not self-seeking. Addiction is none of that! Love is all about grace, not reaching out and caring because it wants something in return. Love gives and gives and gives. Love is at the heart of God's grace.

In grace-based recovery, you begin to see that your true worth is not based on your performance. You take steps toward cleaning up and discover the difficulty of the task, all the many things that must change for you to experience peace and health. But along this path you will discover the most important thing: the love of God and the fellowship of his followers.

If true love is not present in your recovery, then true recovery is not happening. You are worthy of love and you are meant to love others. You must be in a place where you are loved in spite of your past. You must also begin to reach out to love others, breaking free from your old ways of selfishness and pride.

GIVE IT ALL AWAY!

The ultimate goal of grace-based recovery is to give away what has been given to you. True recovery transitions you from a life of taking to one of giving, from serving self to serving others. If you are not eventually giving away your recovery, you might need to question whether you have really been recovering.

This area (giving) is where I see the biggest difference between most recovery programs and a grace-based recovery approach. Most recovery programs are self-focused; if you get what you need, you will be whole and happy. But self-centeredness never leads to real peace and fulfillment.

In fact, if you just look at what addiction trains you to do, you will see the fallacy of self-absorption as a means to happiness. Doesn't addiction teach you to make life all about you, taking whatever you want at any cost to ensure that you are "happy"? But the longer you travel that road, the more you realize that it is a false promise. Addiction, and the self-centeredness that underlies it, only lead to emptiness and loneliness. There is no ultimate satisfaction in that!

Grace-based recovery teaches that because you are already loved, valued, and worth recovery, you no longer have to take and take and take to find your happiness. You can finally rest, knowing that your worth is not dependent on how well you have performed for others. You can give love without strings attached because you can never lose the love God has already given you.

And when you learn to embrace grace, you find yourself motivated to help others. You are gaining a soft heart of compassion, no longer bound to your old, hard heart of selfishness. You begin to care because you have experienced care. You show mercy because you have received mercy.

Jesus told the story of a king whose servant owed him more than he could repay in a lifetime. The king wanted to settle the account, so he summoned the servant and said he would be sold, along with his wife and kids, to repay what he owed. But the servant pleaded for mercy, and the king had compassion on him and forgave his debt.

Afterward, this servant went out and found a guy who owed him the barest fraction of what he owed the king. He demanded that the guy pay up. The guy begged for mercy but the servant refused and instead threw him in jail.

When the king found out what the forgiven servant had done, he was furious. The king responded, "You wicked servant! I forgave you all that debt because you pleaded with me. And should not you have had mercy on your fellow servant, as I had mercy on you?" (Matthew 18:32-33).

You cannot be engaged in true recovery without gaining a heart that grows in compassion for others who are struggling just like you have. Grace will compel you to give away to others who desperately need freedom from their own addictions the insight and wisdom you have gained on your journey. This is the only appropriate response to the freedom and kindness God has shown to you.

> People may excite in themselves a glow of compassion, not
> by toasting their feet at the fire, and saying, "Lord, teach me

compassion," but by going and seeking an object that requires compassion. —Henry Ward Beecher

Grace-based recovery is invitational and warm. It is not a place for people to be beaten up further for their foolish mistakes. It is a place for confession, healing, forgiveness, growth, and compassion. It is an environment of multiplying grace upon grace as those who experience healing and growth freely pass along those gifts to those just starting their recovery journey.

Learn to give away your recovery and you will experience joy like you never thought possible. It truly is better to give than to receive!

DISCUSSION QUESTIONS

1. You were made by God to be fully known and fully loved, as well as to know and love others. What makes this difficult to practice?
2. How is love the fundamental opposite of addiction?
3. Why does making life all about yourself never lead to true contentment? Why is sacrificial love essential to joy?
4. Who do you know that could benefit from what you are learning and experiencing in your recovery? What is preventing you from sharing your life with them?
5. What does "It is better to give than to receive" mean to your recovery?

8

Speaking Blessing over Others

To bless others is to speak words of truth and affirmation over them for the purpose of building them up and encouraging them onward. I can think of no better way to conclude this lesson than to spend some time blessing one another.

Each person takes turns being in the middle of a circle. The rest of the group gathers around while one person speaks the following blessing over them. (Laying hands on the person's shoulders or head is encouraged, if this is desired by the person receiving the blessing.)

> [First Name],
>
> We bless you in the name of Jesus Christ. You are a beloved [son/daughter] of the Most High God, created in him to do good works and to be a blessing to others.
>
> You have been given every spiritual blessing in the heavenly realms to fulfill all that God intended for you. Your life is precious to God; therefore it is precious to us.
>
> May you live this day and every day after in the grace and truth of Jesus for the good of others and the sake of his kingdom,
>
> In the power and promises of God, Amen.

Epilogue:
Hearing God's Voice and Embracing His Grace

As you reflect on these lessons on grace-based recovery, I want to close by sharing two thoughts that I trust will help you integrate these principles into your daily life. First, you must learn to hear God's voice by spending time in his presence. Second, always remember that your worth before God is unchanging.

HEARING GOD'S VOICE

Every addict hears voices. They are like tapes that play in the mind, always telling lies and seducing the addict to go back to what is killing them—over and over and over. These voices got programmed into them early in life and can be very hard to turn off.

God's voice is the only one that really matters in recovery, but his is often very hard to hear. This is not because he doesn't have anything to say or is not talking. It is usually because he speaks softly to those most broken and wearied by sin's deception. This makes it difficult to hear him over all the other noise in life.

There is a great story in the Bible about a prophet named Elijah (1 Kings 18-19). He has a showdown on a mountain with the prophets of the false god, Baal. Both sides were to offer sacrifices to their gods on an altar. Whichever god accepted their sacrifice would be declared the true god for the nation.

The prophets of Baal go first, all 450 of them. They set up their altar and put their sacrifice on it. Then they start crying out to Baal to accept their sacrifice. Nothing. They go on and on, but nothing happens. At one point, Elijah even engages in smack talk, suggesting that their god is sleeping or going to the bathroom. And maybe he was, because nothing happened to the sacrifice they offered.

Finally, they gave up. Then it was Elijah's turn. He set up his altar and placed his sacrifice on it. And to ensure that no one thought he was going to pull off a smoke and mirrors magic act, he built a moat around the base of the altar and drenched everything in water.

Elijah then prayed a simple prayer to God, asking him to accept his sacrifice. The Bible says, "Then the fire of the LORD fell and consumed the burnt offering and the wood and the stones and the dust, and licked up the water that was in the trench" (1 Kings 18:38). Wow! Total victory.

However, in just a matter of days, Elijah was running away in the wilderness, in fear of a queen who was seeking to kill him. It is almost as if he had completely forgotten that the God he served could incinerate rocks and dust. His fear overwhelmed his faith.

But God did not abandon Elijah. He still had more to say and more for him to accomplish. God found Elijah in the wilderness. After caring for his physical needs, God told him to come out of his cave, stand on the mountain, and wait for the Lord to meet him there (1 Kings 19:9-18). Then lots of chaos and noisy stuff started happening.

High winds came by and tore up the rocks, but the Lord wasn't in the wind. After the wind, an earthquake rumbled, but the Lord wasn't in the earthquake. Then a fire raged, but the Lord wasn't in the fire. Finally, after all the noise and commotion, there was the sound of a low whisper, or "thin silence." This is where the Lord was, in the thin silence. Out of this whisper, the Lord gave his next instructions to Elijah.

Recovery is about learning to hear the "low whisper" of God. But to do so requires turning down the noise in life so that you can hear him in the stillness. Turn off the tapes in your head, quiet yourself, and develop the discipline of hearing God. His voice is all that matters, for he is the only one who will never lie to you—ever!

The more you listen to God, the more you will understand the way of grace and more quickly you will recognize the distorted untruths of addiction.

SPEND TIME IN GOD'S PRESENCE

Pull out your calendar and find a block of time (one to three hours minimum) in the next seven to ten days that you can mark off for silence and stillness. Use that time to be still and silent, asking God to meet you in the "thin silence." (Tip: Have your Bible handy in case the Lord wants to lead you to a specific promise or passage.)

EMBRACING GOD'S GRACE

Many recovering addicts have said to me, "Man, I would love to believe what you're saying about grace-based recovery, but it just seems too good. It feels like I would be 'getting away with something' if I really embraced grace. I have always thought recovery is about working my butt off so I don't act out again and I stop disappointing other people."

This is a common response, and one that usually indicates to me that this person is still embracing a fear-based, performance-based recovery paradigm. Neither leads to freedom. Grace sets you free because it shifts the paradigm from thinking that life is all about you (your power, your wisdom, your effort) to understanding what you are really made for: to glorify God.

Addiction sets you up on a self-focused path that eventually wants you to believe that everything in life, including God, needs to revolve around your agenda. When you step into recovery without stepping out of this paradigm, you are destined to simply trade one treadmill (addiction) for another (good works).

Fundamentally, nothing has changed. This is why so many are simply exhausted in recovery. They are not free because they still think it is all about them working, working, working in order to *earn* their freedom. But by God's grace, no one earns their freedom; it is a *free gift*!

Does this sound too good to be true? Can you really *receive* freedom rather than work like a dog for it? Isn't this just an excuse for people who are too lazy to work hard in recovery?

Make no mistake, grace-based recovery is *not* about encouraging a person to continue acting out. It is about teaching them that their value and purpose are not wrapped up in their performance. *Your value as a human being is not equal to what you do!* This is the critical step toward understanding and embracing God's grace; your free gift to freedom.

Don't try to impress anyone in recovery. That is connecting your worth to your works. You are broken, sinful, and in need of great help in order to become who you were made by God to be. Do not be afraid of your brokenness. Embrace it and allow the grace of God to lead you to places of insight, integrity, and service.

God's grace is so good that you can never outrun it. You cannot fail so much that grace can't pick you up. You cannot work so hard that grace can't lead you to a place of rest. You cannot lie, hide, cheat, or rebel so badly that grace can't bring you back. Your brokenness cannot overwhelm God's grace!

So why not live every day in this grace and learn to grow by it? You won't regret it!

Leader Guide

Introduction
Grace-Based Recovery: A Safe Place to Heal and Grow

Main idea: Creating a safe, healing environment [5 min]

Bible passage: Matthew 11:28-30 [10 min]

GBR article: A safe place to heal [10 min]

Discussion questions [15 min]

Group exercise [15-20 min]

Leader guide: We are laying the groundwork in this introduction for the entire series on grace-based recovery. It's all about the environment; the group setting matters when communicating the God-given value of every person present. This introduction will help unpack how grace establishes a safe, healing environment and why this is so critical to recovery.

SETUP: The two environments that we will be comparing throughout this study are grace-based groups and performance-based groups. Grace-based recovery measures a person's value by the intrinsic worth he or she is given by God as a human being made in his image. Performance-based recovery measures a person's value by the quality and consistency of his or her behavior. We will seek to establish that a grace-based recovery environment is far superior in helping people break free from addiction to live holy, fruitful lives in the Lord.

Begin the session by reading the Main Idea and the Bible Passage together.

MAIN IDEA

Grace-based recovery is about creating a safe, healing environment for overcoming addictions and strongholds[1] of any kind. The atmosphere of a grace-based environment is welcoming and open, inviting broken sinners to find their hope and healing in Jesus Christ, not in the strength of their own will.

BIBLE PASSAGE

Matthew 11:28-30

"Come to me, all who labor and are heavy laden, and I will give you rest. Take my yoke upon you, and learn from me, for I am gentle and lowly in heart, and you will find rest for your souls. For my yoke is easy, and my burden is light."

ASK: What makes addictive patterns so exhausting? Why is there no rest in the ongoing pursuit of more?

ASK: In this Bible passage, how does Jesus instruct us to receive rest? What instruction does he give for us to find rest? What is the difference? *[Point out the passive nature of receiving grace (Jesus "gives" us rest) and the active nature of applying that grace (we must "take" Christ's yoke upon us) in experiencing deeper rest.]*

---

1. When the term "addiction" is used in this study, it primarily refers to compulsive, destructive behaviors. When the term "stronghold" is used, it primarily refers to spiritual and emotional bondage to false beliefs about yourself, God, and life.

ASK: How does a grace-based environment for recovery encourage you to face your addiction? What does "resting in Christ" mean to the recovery process?

TRANSITION TO ARTICLE: The safer the environment to heal, the more likely you will be to open up about your struggles and failures. Let's read this lesson's article to give us a better idea of what this safe environment could look like.

Read the article aloud together and then go over the discussion questions.

Introduction

A Safe Place to Heal

"Hi. Welcome to the group. My name is Jonathan."

"Hi. I'm Joe."

"I'm glad you're here, Joe. We'll get started in a few minutes. Help yourself to some coffee and grab a seat in the circle. Hey guys, this is Joe."

In unison, "Hi, Joe!"

If you are Joe, this can be a terrifying experience, right? On the one hand, it is wonderful to be greeted, reassured that you are in the right place, and actually welcomed. On the other hand, it is frightening because everybody knows why you are there. You are addicted. Ouch!

As scary as this scene may be, you must enter it if there is going to be any hope for freedom from your addiction. You must enter a place where you are accepted in all your brokenness, a place where healing is available and transformation is waiting. You must *enter*.

Grace-based recovery is a safe place

Grace-based environments often come in the form of a support group or small-group counseling or coaching. They are places where your full story can be heard without judgment or shame. In such an atmosphere, you are loved and embraced because of your *presence*, not because of your *performance*. It is safe to be real in a grace-based group.

Grace is an often misunderstood and misapplied concept. **Grace is simply defined as undeserved favor or kindness**. When you are offered grace, it is a free gift of acceptance and kindness that is not dependent on your goodness or behavior. It is a gift that validates your worth as a human being *because you are a human being.*

When you step into a grace-based recovery environment for the first time, it might feel a bit awkward, like you are in a foreign country. Is it really a place where you aren't condemned? A place where your worth isn't based on your performance? A place where joy, truth, and acceptance are offered with no strings? I know it seems too good to be true. It *is* good, but it's also true—grace is out there!

> "Joe, why don't you share some of your story with us? Tell us why you're here."
>
> "Well, are you sure you want to hear it? I mean, it's pretty bad. I've done some really stupid, hurtful things that I'm ashamed of. Is it really okay to share that here?"
>
> "Joe, we like to call this a 'No Shame Zone' (or NSZ for short). That means that no matter what you share, we won't stand in condemnation over you. Heck, we're just like you! We want you to share your story because until you do, you won't be able to start the journey of recovery to a whole new you."
>
> "Okay. Here goes . . ."

The foundation of a grace-based recovery environment is the invitation from Jesus in Matthew 11:28, "Come to me, all who labor and are heavy laden, and I will give you rest." This invitation is a call to both the self-righteous do-gooder and the desperate outcast to make their way to Jesus. In Jesus, there is rest for the weary; his grace invites you into his rest. And no one needs grace and rest more than the one who is addicted.

Do you want rest for your weary soul? Do you want a place where you can heal and grow? Then you need grace-based recovery, a place where your value is constant and your life matters to God. Take on the easy yoke and light burden of Jesus and you will discover the rest he promises.

Grace-based recovery is a healing place

Grace-based recovery means learning how to live in freedom every day. No one will do recovery perfectly, but perfection isn't the point. Healing and growth are what this journey is all about. Grace is the vehicle that moves you from a self-centered addict to a loving child of God.

Attitude in recovery is huge. Grace offers a vision of hope. No matter how far you have fallen in your addiction, grace always meets you there to pick you up. When you know that you have value, that *you are worth recovery*, you just might be able to take that first step and tell your story. You just might be able to start seeing yourself a little differently than before. You might start recovering and establishing a foundation for a whole new life.

If I gave you an acorn and told you to plant it today, would you expect to see a full-grown oak tree tomorrow? Of course not! There is a (long) process of growth that must occur before a tiny acorn becomes a massive oak. But the ultimate purpose of that acorn was always to become an oak tree. In the same way, your ultimate purpose has always been to be an "oak of righteousness" that bears God's holy image in his world (Isaiah 61:1-3). The seed of grace planted in you today will mature over time into a flourishing life of freedom and joy.

Grace-based environments give you the time and space to "grow up" in recovery. It takes time to unpack your whole story and start moving in a new direction. You need an environment where such time and patience are offered. That is grace-based recovery.

> "Joe, I sure hope we see you again soon."
> "Oh, I'm sure I'll be back. This is the best I've felt in years."
> "Well, just so you know, even if we don't see you for another six months, you're still welcome here. You are always welcome here."

Leader guide: The main points of the article are: Grace creates safety (your worth is intrinsic; it is built in to your design, not something you have to earn) and grace promotes healing (you have time to engage in the long, messy process of recovery because your worth before God is unchanging). Be sure to emphasize this before going on to the discussion questions.

Go over Questions 1-3 in group. Encourage group members to ponder and answer Questions 4-5 on their own.

Allow your time on Question 3 to set up the group exercise of sharing specific fears that keep us from opening up about weaknesses and failures.

DISCUSSION QUESTIONS

1. How can you identify with Joe's experience of stepping into a group for the first time? Why is a grace-based environment so important in that first encounter?
2. In a grace-based environment "you are loved and embraced because of your *presence*, not because of your *performance*." How does this idea make you feel? How does such an environment motivate you toward recovery?
3. What might make it difficult to enter a grace-based recovery environment?
4. How does a grace-based recovery environment change your perspective on the time frame it might take for real change and transformation to take place in your life? Does this encourage or discourage you? Why?
5. Is anything preventing you from coming to Jesus to find rest? If so, what is it? What would it take for you to let it go?

Leader guide: This exercise is an opportunity to "practice what we preach." Can we demonstrate what a No-Shame-Zone really looks like? Make sure to lay the ground rules of respect, brevity, and non-preachiness. (Refer to "A Word to Group Leaders," p. ix) This exercise is meant to highlight the value of a grace-based environment by affirming the God-given worth of every member, no matter how broken or sinful their behavior.

Gently correct if affirming statements from the group are not aligned with truth (i.e., if someone affirms a sinful behavior or proclaims a false identity over someone, such as "It's okay, you were born that way," referring to any sinful pattern).

As the group leader, it might be best for you to share first to set the example and illustrate how the exercise is to be done.

Introduction

Celebrate God!

Since this is a NSZ (No-Shame-Zone), share any fear you have about opening up to others about your weaknesses and failures. After each person shares, other members of the group are invited to make one affirming comment to the person who shared. (Be respectful, brief, and non-preachy.)

If you prefer not to participate verbally, simply say "Pass" when it is your turn. But consider allowing other members to speak affirming words over you, whether or not they know your specific fears. The truth spoken over you is powerful in breaking spiritual and emotional strongholds and affirming God's message of grace and love.

> **Leader guide:** Wrap up the meeting with prayer and a word of encouragement.

1

Grace to Overcome

Main idea: Grace-based paradigm vs. performance-based paradigm

Bible passage: Titus 2:11-14

GBR article: Grace changes everything!

Discussion questions

Group exercise: Celebrate God!

Leader guide: Since grace is the foundation of true recovery, it is important that you establish a good working definition for "grace." Here is the one we use: "Grace" is God's undeserved and unearned favor or kindness. The key to understanding grace is to know that it is a gift; there is no way to earn grace. There is no such thing as "getting credit for what you've done" with grace. Instead, grace-based recovery is a journey of receiving God's gift of freedom and wholeness rather than attempting to earn it. This may take a while for those entering recovery to fully understand (probably longer than this study will last). Be patient but persistent in conveying this definition of grace and its application to recovery.

  SETUP: Definitions matter. It is important to understand what grace is and how it relates to recovery. This lesson is about helping us understand this connection and how it applies to us personally in our recovery.

Read the Main idea and Bible passage together.

MAIN IDEA

Grace is essential for overcoming addictive strongholds—the compulsive behaviors and false beliefs that have ensnared you. The fact that God offers you grace shows you that you have value to God; it's a value that isn't based on your performance. Grace is God's unearned favor or kindness toward you. You and I don't deserve God's love, but he offers it to us by grace. Therefore, recovery is more of a gift from God than it is a reward for your good performance.

Real recovery isn't just about *not* doing something wrong or unhealthy; it's about living daily in connection with God and others, and learning to live according to his Word. It isn't based on your skill or willpower; it's based on the grace of God. You must receive this gift of grace[1] and let it work in your life if you are ever to break free from addictive strongholds.

BIBLE PASSAGE

Titus 2:11-14

> For the grace of God has appeared, bringing salvation for all people, **training us to renounce ungodliness and worldly passions, and to live self-controlled, upright, and godly lives in the present age**, waiting for our blessed hope, the appearing of the glory of our great God and Savior Jesus Christ, who gave himself for us to redeem us from all lawlessness and to purify for himself a people for his own possession who are zealous for good works. (author's emphasis)

---

1. See "For Group Members: Before You Get Started" to learn how you can receive God's free gift of grace and eternal life.

Leader guide:

ASK: How does grace reveal that we have value to God? And how does grace make this value unchanging? *[Suggested answer: The fact that God offers forgiveness for our sins when we deserve judgment is a clear indicator that God values our lives. And because this gift of forgiveness and life comes from God and cannot be earned by us, it reveals the unchangeable nature of our value to him. He is unchanging, and our value to him is unchanging. He expressed his love to us through the death of Jesus Christ on our behalf. He offers forgiveness of sins to all who trust in him, and his resurrection opens the door to new life for those who believe in him. His grace proves his love for us, and he doesn't change his mind.]*

ASK: In the Titus passage, what is "training us"? How is this different from what we might normally think "trains" us in recovery? *[Suggested answer: What is the difference between a "law-based" recovery and a "grace-based" one? These two questions are addressing the conflict between performance-based recovery and grace-based recovery. According to Titus 2:11, it is grace that trains us, not law. Challenge group members to think through the differences between grace and law from a relational perspective. Law can be quite non-relational, simply turning recovery and life into a list that one completes alone.]*

ASK: What does grace train us against and what does it train us for, according to Titus 2:12? How do you see this combination of resisting and pursuing worked out in the recovery process?

TRANSITION TO ARTICLE: If we don't have grace as the strong foundation to our recovery, we will naturally drift toward a performance-based path. Let's read this article aloud together to better understand how grace changes everything.

Lesson

1

ARTICLE

Grace Changes Everything!

Recovery from any addiction is hard. (What an understatement, right?) But sometimes it is made even harder by programs intended to help you break free from your compulsions. Some programs can make you feel as if an additional burden is being laid onto your already heavy heart. And even if a program is well-meaning, the message that can be communicated is, "If you don't measure up to the standards of our program, you will be seen as an even greater failure." This doesn't make for a good start to an already daunting journey.

Grace offers a different approach to recovery, one that doesn't place your value on the ever-changing roller coaster of performance. Grace gives hope to the person just realizing the need for recovery, and also breathes new life into the one who has been on the journey a while but feels stuck in a rigid rut of rules and performance-based rituals.

Grace-based recovery offers a pathway to true healing and lifelong freedom. Such recovery isn't merely about managing behaviors or simply "not acting out." It provides a way to experience fullness in every aspect of life and a pursuit of purpose that is meaningful and joyous.

I have experienced many different kinds of recovery programs since 1999, when all my secrets[2] and lies came to the surface. I have tried many

---

2. Read my full story in my book, *Secrets* (NewGrowthPress.com/Secrets).

methods, from "pain therapy" to intense Bible study and militaristic accountability.[3] I have read many books, worked with numerous counselors, attended seminars, and studied multiple curriculums on addiction recovery.

Over all these years, I have found very few, if any, resources that are grace-based. Most are what I refer to as "sin management systems," a way to feel better about yourself and your failures without ever truly breaking free. It is sad. But it is not unfixable!

Do you want to be free from your addiction? Of course you do! Addiction sucks. Literally. It sucks the life from you. It tears apart relationships, destroys character, weakens the body, depresses the soul, and ultimately leads to death—in all areas of life. *No one sets out to become addicted.* But once you find yourself drowning in addiction, you must make a difficult choice: enter recovery or get worse.

Entering recovery is not easy. It means having to admit things about yourself that are embarrassing and ugly. It means that someone else will have to hear your story of brokenness, selfishness, foolish decisions, and lack of self-control. You will have to decide if the pain of recovery is worth more than the continued, worsening pain of addiction.

You might lose your reputation if you choose recovery, because now the truth is out. You might lose your spouse. You might lose your children, your job, your possessions, even your life. Although you might lose such things if you choose recovery, it is more likely that you would lose those things *anyway* if you continue down the path of addiction. Any losses in recovery cannot compare with what is ultimately gained: freedom, peace, and joy.

But you might be wondering, *How can grace cause all this change?* I realize that the idea of grace doesn't seem to fit with our normal understanding (or experience) with recovery. We think of recovery in terms of delivering

---

3. This book is not intended to attack any particular method of recovery, but rather to expose possible fallacies of underlying performance-based principles that are counter to grace-based recovery.

brutal confessions, agonizing amend-making, setting up stringent boundaries, keeping high levels of accountability, and working our butts off. And while all those things are very much a part of the recovery process, apart from grace they simply become an idolatrous task list that exhausts the body and soul almost as much as addiction.

Grace changes everything because grace gives you a new lens through which to see the whole process of recovery. Grace reminds you over and over again that your value before God is unchanging regardless of your bad (or good) performance. Grace invites you to an ongoing process of growth in the context of love, joy, and authentic community.

Here are some possible differences between a grace-based perspective and a performance-based perspective and how they might affect recovery.

Grace-Based Recovery	Performance-Based Recovery
Personal value is a constant.	Personal value fluctuates, based on behavior.
Confession explores mistakes to learn and grow from them.	Confession punishes bad behavior by a "start over" mentality.
Accountability is an opportunity to build others up in truth and love.	Accountability is a tool to control or force behavioral outcomes.
Allows for safe exploration of wounds, shame, false beliefs, etc.	Focuses on behavior over and above the emotional.
Grace leads to humility.	Performance leads to pride.
Grace shifts focus to God and others.	Performance focuses on me.
Grace sets people free.	Performance manages sin.

I know that this chart can be troubling for some, especially those who have had experiences in highly behaviorally focused programs. My intent is not to upset. I know that many have found help and significant breakthroughs in such settings. But there is no denying the differences between a recovery setting that is primarily focused on behavior modification (performance-based) and one that is focused on the freedom that God desires to give (grace-based)—even if those differences don't play out exactly the way the chart describes.

I have worked with hundreds of addicted individuals over the years and all who have come from performance-based environments have expressed the same sentiment: even after eliminating their addictive behaviors, something was still missing. They still felt "unfree" from something. In other words, simply "not acting out" was not real freedom, not true recovery. This is where grace must enter the journey. Without the favor and kindness of God, there is no freedom, even if you never act out again.

Spend some time asking God to show you his grace. Open yourself up to this wonderful gift. Read and reread Titus 2:11-14 and ask God to show you how he wants to manifest his grace in your life and recovery. Don't rush this conversation. Sit in grace and let it soak to your bones. Be enveloped by the truth that in Jesus Christ, your value to God is unchangeable—he really does love you! When that truth sinks deep into your soul, you will know the grace of God—and it will change everything.

> **Leader guide:** This article is trying to help the reader connect the definition of grace to the recovery process and to see how this contrasts with a performance-based model. Try to bring clarity to these connections before entering into the discussion questions. Deal graciously with anyone who might be upset over the chart of differences and explore where their discomfort about it might be originating.
>
> After reading the article aloud together, go over the discussion questions.
>
> Go over questions 1-3 together as a group. Camp out on question 3 and explore the necessity of humility in a grace-based recovery process; this is a reason why it's so hard to embrace. Grace doesn't allow us to take credit for anything good that comes from recovery (this will dovetail with the Group exercise). Encourage group members to respond to Question 4 on their own, suggesting that they journal about it.
>
> Allow your time on Question 3 to set up the group exercise of confession and surrender.

DISCUSSION QUESTIONS

1. Define "grace." Why is God's grace so important to your personal recovery?

2. Thinking about all that you could lose as a result of your addiction, share your top reasons for why you are committed to recovery. Now ask yourself if those reasons are grounded in your relationship with God or in your own ability and strength. How can you move more toward a grace motivation (following God's instruction and lead) rather than a performance motivation (following your own wisdom and ideas)?

3. Why is a grace-based recovery approach actually hard to practice? What is required in order to truly receive (embrace) grace? (Hint: Think of the differences between humility and pride.)

4. Review the chart of differences between Grace-Based and Performance-Based recovery. Where in your own recovery have you seen more of a performance-based approach rather than grace-based? How can you take more of a grace-based approach moving forward?

1

**GROUP
EXERCISE**

Celebrate God!

In grace-based recovery, all celebrations of victory give the credit to God rather than yourself. Why? Because recovery is a *gift* of God's grace. Therefore, he deserves the glory, not you. This kind of celebrating can be difficult to do, when it feels very much like you were the one who resisted the temptation to act out! But remember, it is *grace* that trains us "to renounce ungodliness and worldly passions." Even victories are a gift of God's grace.

Go around the group and share a victory from the past week. Keeping in mind that victories are gifts from God, share how this changes your perspective and attitude toward the specific victory you shared. Spend time together celebrating God for giving you all you needed to resist temptation and "live self-controlled, upright, and godly" in that moment.

> **Leader guide:** This lesson emphasizes the necessity of understanding grace to appreciate one's personal value to God. It also shows how this truth provides a new lens through which to see the entire process of recovery. The group exercise is meant to emphasize this lens and help members see that even victories are a gracious gift from God, not the result of their own power or wisdom. Help members to see the value and need for celebrating (worshipping) God for the full impact of his grace in recovery and growth. Such an attitude of celebration will serve them well as they navigate more advanced stages of recovery.
>
> Wrap up the meeting with prayer and a word of encouragement.

2

Grace to Share Your Story

Main idea: Tell your story, tell the truth

Bible passage: 1 John 1:5-10

GBR article: Telling the truth about yourself

Discussion questions

Group exercise: How to tell the truth (the truth, the whole truth, nothing but the truth)

Leader guide: The first kind of "confession" that is necessary in recovery is for the addicted individual to tell his or her story—the full story. This sounds simple and makes sense, but it is very daunting for the person carrying the secrets. This is why a grace-based environment is so critical. You as the leader must set the tone for inviting stories of brokenness to be told. You also need to establish how such stories are to be told—what is necessary to share and what is unnecessary. We will get to this in the group exercise.

SETUP: To invite people to tell their stories in a recovery setting, you need to ensure that the stories told are connected to why they are in the recovery setting. In other words, if the group is to help people recover from alcohol abuse, the story needs to describe how and when those patterns of addiction formed, not the person's high school athletic record or the like (unless it directly relates to their addiction story).

Here are key elements for group members to share when telling their stories:

- Their first exposure to the substance or behavior they struggle with now.
- What happened next, and when they began willfully participating in their addictive behavior.
- Thoughts and feelings they had about what they were doing throughout the entire progression of their addiction.
- Thoughts and feelings they had about themselves throughout the entire progression of their addiction.
- The effect their addiction had on relationships and their ability to function in society.
- The nature of their relationship with God throughout their story.
- Their hopes and dreams for a life free from addiction.

Read the Main idea and Bible passage together.

MAIN IDEA

The effect of God's grace is only fully realized when you bring your unfiltered story of brokenness into the light. You cannot keep your story hidden and expect to be transformed into a new person who is free from strongholds. Your *full* story must be told. It is the key step to "walking in the light" and beginning the healing journey of recovery.

BIBLE PASSAGE

1 John 1:5-10

This is the message we have heard from him and proclaim to you, that God is light, and in him is no darkness at all. If we say we have fellowship with him while we walk in darkness, we lie and do not practice the truth. But if we walk in the light, as he is in the light, we have fellowship with one another, and the blood of Jesus his Son cleanses us from all sin. If we say we have no sin, we deceive ourselves, and the truth is not in us. If we confess our sins, he is faithful and just to forgive us our sins and to cleanse us from all unrighteousness. If we say we have not sinned, we make him a liar, and his word is not in us.

ASK: What scares you about confessing your full story of sin and brokenness? How does the idea of a grace-based environment help to lessen those fears?

ASK: In the passage from 1 John, there is a contrast made between light and darkness, where light represents God and truth and darkness is associated with sin and deception. Paint a word picture using this imagery to describe what telling your story must look like.

ASK: What do you see in this Scripture passage that speaks not only to "coming clean" before God but also the effect of confession on relationships with others? What does "walking in the light" and "fellowship with one another" look like?

Leader guide: The following article invites group members to consider what it means to tell their full story in a grace-based environment, acknowledging the difficulty of such an invitation. Telling the truth is not a simple "flip of the switch" for someone who has been living in secret lies for a long time. It is important for group members to understand the challenges involved in telling their story, but also the necessity of telling it if they ever want to experience true recovery and freedom.

TRANSITION TO ARTICLE: If we believe that our value to God is based on our performance rather than his grace, how can we ever truly open up about our full story? Grace invites us to step into the light and leave behind the self-centered deception that keeps us trapped in our sin and secrecy.

Let's read the article aloud together.

ARTICLE

2

Telling the Truth about Yourself

You can never break free from addiction without telling the truth—the whole truth! God's grace covers your sin but never excuses it. To lie in recovery is to turn 180 degrees and walk right back into the darkness you want to flee. Addiction is a house of lies and the only way to tear down lies is with the truth. Therefore, you must tell someone your story of brokenness.

Grace-based recovery invites you to tell your full story, because there is nothing that you could reveal that God does not already know. Honesty is about building your character and learning how to "walk in the light," no longer willing to carry around secrets that slowly snuff out your life.

I must admit that this is a difficult challenge. Addicts are pros when it comes to lying; it is how the addiction stays hidden and perpetuates. This is why it is so difficult to come out of the dark and tell your full story. To be known is a risk.

I remember vividly the first time I was encouraged by my counselor to step into a support group and share my story. It was only a few weeks after I began meeting with this counselor. I felt terror. I had shared my story with the counselor but it felt safe because he was bound by law not to retell my story to anyone else. But now I was being invited to share with people who didn't come with that same kind of legal protection. I was scared. But I did it. And I'm glad I did. My life has never been the same since.

By definition, "walking in the light" will expose whatever you have been carrying in the dark. And because what you have been carrying in the dark is exactly what you have been trying to hide, it will be painful to bring it into the light. But if you never tell your full story, you will never experience full freedom.

Grace-based recovery gives you the courage to do difficult things so that you might discover God's best for your life.

GRACE-BASED RECOVERY ACCEPTS YOUR STORY OF BROKENNESS

Oftentimes, recovery programs become so focused on moving an addict forward to places of cleaned-up behavior and radical lifestyle changes that they fail to embrace or accept the brokenness of the person in front of them. Grace embraces you, *all* of you.

Sometimes this level of acceptance is hard to receive. You have probably beaten yourself up so much and immersed yourself in shame for so long that to have someone invite you to tell your story and not shun you as a result might feel shocking. But it is necessary to let others into your story, into the broken places where you have been wounded, lied to, and calloused. It is okay to feel awkward in the presence of grace, but I assure you that, over time, it will become your favorite place to be. It is the place where community, love, and godly character exist and grow.

Many people assume that grace would be easy to receive. But so few have experienced real grace-filled environments, they don't actually have a clue as to whether it would be easy or not. Then, when they do enter a grace-based environment, they are hit with the shock that it wasn't as easy as they assumed to receive the free gift of complete, unmerited acceptance.

If it takes you a while to warm up to the idea that others (even God) could receive you this way, be patient with yourself. Everybody who enters into grace-based recovery squirms at first. Many spend a lot of energy trying to prove themselves worthy, pointing out all the good things they have started to do in recovery in an attempt to feel like they did something to earn the gift of grace. But that is not how grace works. It is free!

God knew your story—all of it—before you were born. All your sin. All your failures. All your shame. And yet he chose to make a way for you to be connected to him forever through the life, death, and resurrection of Jesus Christ. When you trust in Christ for the forgiveness of your sins, you are given eternal life with God. May this glorious gift of grace from God give you the confidence to tell your story to someone else!

GRACE-BASED RECOVERY ALWAYS LEAVES THE DOOR OPEN

You will not "walk in the light" perfectly. You will stumble on this journey of recovery. So how does a grace-based group respond when the unfolding of each member's story is rough and imperfect?

There is no "three-strikes-and-you're-out" in grace-based recovery. Grace always welcomes home the stray addict. Always! If we truly want to see lives changed and addicts set free, we can never close the door on one another, no matter how often or for how long we might fall. Grace cannot be measured. (After all, how can you quantify something that is free?) Grace can only be poured out.

In Luke 15 there is a great story about a son who is selfish and arrogant. He squanders his father's wealth in a foreign country and eventually finds himself starving to death in a pig pen. Finally, broken and exhausted over his sin, he returns to his father to see if he can just be one of the servants in his house. But his dad sees him coming down the road and sprints to embrace him, kiss him, and throw a party for his return. This boy was not rejected when he came crawling home. He was met with grace from a loving father. This is what grace-based recovery must look like for the wayward addict.

When an addict falls in recovery (notice I said *when*) and repents, he must be allowed back into the group. If he is left outside, it will only reinforce a performance-based recovery that strictly sees a person's value to the group in terms of his behavior. But grace sees the addict's value regardless of behavior. And besides, it is *inside* the group where the returning addict will get the help needed to keep moving toward recovery, healing, and wholeness.

Is grace-based recovery what you want? Then jump in. Tell your full story, and keep telling your story as it unfolds in the light of God's faithful grace. And never forget that God is keenly interested in your story—all of it!

> **Leader guide:** After reading the article aloud together, go over the discussion questions. Give each member the homework assignment of writing out their story using the guidelines provided at the beginning of this lesson. Then, for the remainder of this Grace-based recovery study, invite one or two willing members each meeting to share their story. Allow seven to eight minutes per story.

DISCUSSION QUESTIONS

1. What scares you the most about being fully known? How do you typically respond to such fears?
2. Respond to this statement: *If you never tell your full story, you will never experience full freedom.* Why is this true?
3. Is "telling your story" a one-time event? Why is it important to continue telling your story throughout your recovery and growth?
4. What are some positive effects of telling your full story to safe people? (*Suggested answers: it fosters humility, exposes areas that need work, invites friendship, etc.*)
5. How can you overcome the shame that fights against you telling your full story?

> **Leader guide:** Allow your time on Question 3 to set up the group exercise of how to tell the truth.

Lesson

2

GROUP EXERCISE

How to Tell the Truth

Telling your story is an exercise in telling the truth about yourself. But addiction teaches you the opposite: how to lie about (and to) yourself. This means that a huge part of recovery is simply learning how to tell the truth. I know it sounds ridiculous, but when you have been so conditioned by addict-thinking, it can be more difficult than you realize to simply speak truthfully—about anything!

A simple way to begin speaking more truthfully is to ask yourself these three questions before opening your mouth:

1. Is it true? In other words, is it factual?
2. Is it the whole truth? Are you trying to leave anything out or are you declaring the full reality?
3. Is it nothing but the truth? Are you embellishing or adding to the facts?

As your group exercise, do the following. Think of one thing that happened in your life in the last twenty-four to forty-eight hours. It can be anything; it doesn't have to be related to recovery. Share what happened and how it made you feel, filtering the occurrence through the three questions above (Truth, Whole Truth, Nothing but the Truth). Then discuss with one another how you think this exercise will help you become a more truthful person.

> **Leader guide:** This lesson is about inviting individuals to come out of the dark and into the light with their story of brokenness.

This is often a scary proposition and one that tempts people to not tell the truth, the whole truth, and nothing but the truth. This is why a grace-based environment is so critical to this storytelling. The people sharing need to know that their worth is permanently established by the life, death, and resurrection of Jesus. This affords them the freedom to unpack their story.

Encourage the members hearing the stories to be gracious and empathetic with any questions they may have about someone's story. The Golden Rule is the best rule to abide by in grace-based recovery.

Wrap up the meeting with prayer and a word of encouragement.

Lesson

3

Grace to Belong

Main idea: Authentic community, healing wounds

Bible passages: Ecclesiastes 4:9-12; John 15:12-17

GBR article: Where healing and growth happen

Discussion questions

Group exercise: Making friends (more than one-dimensional)

Leader guide: Most addicts feel as if they are unique in their brokenness and therefore don't fit anywhere. But it is precisely their brokenness that makes them a fit for a recovery community, because everyone present is broken in some way. Rather than getting distracted with all the specific differences in how everyone's brokenness may be expressed in behavior, it is important to focus on the similarities, not merely of brokenness but of need. We are all more alike than we are different and we all have the same need: recovery (or redemption). Let's embrace the community of recovery and discover that, by God's grace, we all have a place to belong.

   SETUP: Most who enter recovery do not have any real friends. They have family and some even have lots of acquaintances, but no true friends who know them fully. Since true recovery is not just about stopping behavior, it is important to establish that being known and loved is essential for lifelong freedom from addictive strongholds. It is only through authentic community that we learn and live out what "loving God" and "loving your neighbor" is all about (Mark 12:28-31). This is really the ultimate mission of recovery.

Read the Main idea and Bible passage together.

MAIN IDEA

Addiction leads to loneliness. It has a way of driving people out of your life because addiction is so self-focused. There is little room for empathy or care for others in addiction. Therefore, recovery is a process of learning how to live and thrive in community—real community, not merely being around people. You need people who know and love you. You also need people you can know and love. You need a place to belong. And grace-based recovery creates such environments.

BIBLE PASSAGES

Ecclesiastes 4:9-12

Two are better than one, because they have a good reward for their toil. For if they fall, one will lift up his fellow. But woe to him who is alone when he falls and has not another to lift him up! Again, if two lie together, they keep warm, but how can one keep warm alone? And though a man might prevail against one who is alone, two will withstand him—a threefold cord is not quickly broken.

John 15:12-17

"This is my commandment, that you love one another as I have loved you. Greater love has no one than this, that someone lay down his life for his friends. You are my friends if you do what I command you. No longer do I call you servants, for the servant does not know what his master is doing; but I have called you friends, for all that I have heard from my Father I have made known to you. You did not choose me, but I chose you and appointed you that you should go and bear fruit and that your fruit should abide, so that whatever you ask the Father in my name, he may give it to you. These things I command you, so that you will love one another."

ASK: Who is the last person you could point to in your life as a true best friend? Can you define what a "best friend" really means?

ASK: What do you think Jesus meant when he said, "Love one another as I have loved you?" How did Jesus love us? How does addiction keep us from loving others like Jesus loved us?

ASK: How does addictive thinking and behaving drive us away from friendship and authentic community?

This lesson's article invites group members to examine their history of wounds and recognize their need for healing, along with the fact that such healing can only come through true community. No one heals from anything without needing others, yet so many try to face their addiction alone. Until addicts embrace true community as the environment where healing and growth occurs, they will remain enslaved or, at best, limping along.

TRANSITION TO ARTICLE: Recovery is about healing and growth: healing from past wounds and false thinking; growth in God's grace and truth. But none of this occurs in a vacuum. Community is the environment of healing and growth.

Read the article aloud together.

3

Where Healing and Growth Happen

Most addicts believe recovery is for the sole purpose of correcting out-of-control compulsions. If you are a drug addict or an alcoholic, recovery will help you stop drinking or doing drugs. If you are a sex or food addict, recovery will help you stop acting out sexually or overeating. This is the "healing" most addicts seek in recovery. But that is not what needs healing.

Jesus spent a lot of time in his ministry correcting religious leaders for their misunderstanding and distortion of God's instructions. They tended to look at God's law and interpret it strictly on a behavioral level; what does it tell us to do (or not do)? Jesus even suggested that they flawlessly performed the letter of the law (Matthew 5:20), while they grossly missed the heart of it.

> He [Jesus] went on from there and entered their synagogue. And a man was there with a withered hand. And they asked him, "Is it lawful to heal on the Sabbath?"—so that they might accuse him. He said to them, "Which one of you who has a sheep, if it falls into a pit on the Sabbath, will not take hold of it and lift it out? Of how much more value is a man than a sheep! So it is lawful to do good on the Sabbath." Then he said to the man, "Stretch out your hand." And the man stretched it out, and it was restored, healthy like the other. But the Pharisees went out and conspired against him, how to destroy him. (Matthew 12:9-14)

These Pharisees knew the letter of the law—that one shouldn't "work" on the Sabbath— but they totally missed the heart of it. Jesus exposed these men for their hypocrisy and lack of compassion. Their rigid adherence to the rules created hard hearts that sought more to control others than to care for them. Jesus, on the other hand, showed them the heart of the law, that "it is lawful to do good on the Sabbath."

When Jesus healed that guy's hand, do you think the healed man cared what day of the week it was? Neither did Jesus. At the heart of God's law is love. Jesus didn't break the law by healing this man; he embodied the law, the law of love.

If you are addicted to something, you have a history of being wounded. Some of your wounds may be physical, other wounds are emotional or verbal, possibly even spiritual. These wounds often become a foundational element of what eventually led you toward addiction. There is no such thing as an unscarred addict.

The wounds in your soul need healing. When you share your full story, these wounds will come to the surface, and the pain you feel today may be just as powerful as when you were first hurt. But Jesus can carry you through the pain to a place of healing and restoration in your soul. You do not have to continue living under the weight of unhealed wounds.

God's grace helps you heal by reminding you that you are worth saving; you are worth your recovery. Some may say that because of what you have done, you aren't worth saving. You should rot in hell or at least be made to suffer for what you have done. But God sees beyond your acting out and looks at the wounded soul inside, the little child who was neglected, beaten, raped, left to fend for himself, or was never good enough. God sees your brokenness and offers you a pathway to healing.

It takes time to heal from deep wounds in your soul. You must be patient with yourself. You must examine areas of your heart that have probably been hidden for a long time. You need grace, not law, to encourage you to keep going when you grow weary and want to give up. Grace offers you time, however long it takes to heal.

COMMUNITY IS WHERE HEALING THRIVES

It is one thing to know that your wounds need healing. It is another thing entirely to actually begin the healing process. While this study will not address all the facets of that process, it is important that we direct you to the environment where the healing effects of grace thrive: Christ-centered, Christ-empowered community.

The entire point of this grace-based recovery study is that we need safe, grace-filled environments to unpack our brokenness and pursue God's best for our lives. Essential to this process is community—the fellowship, encouragement, and accountability of other Christ-followers, who know what it is to be known, forgiven, and made new by Jesus. You will never experience the fullness of healing (physical, emotional, and spiritual) in isolation. God designed you to belong—to him and to other Christ-followers. We need each other if we are to heal and grow in our recovery.

When I think about the importance of community to healing in recovery, the image that comes to mind is that of a hospital. If you broke your leg, you would not assume that such an injury could heal without the involvement of others. You would need someone to transport you to professional help. You would need a doctor or surgeon to assess the damage and prescribe the right treatment. You would need nurses, pharmacists, physical therapists, and more to walk you through (no pun intended) all the stages in the healing of your broken leg. In addition, you would need the emotional support of friends and family and the spiritual support of the Holy Spirit and your church family. You would need community to heal from a broken leg.

So ask yourself this question: how much *more* do you think you need a Christ-centered community to heal from the wounds connected to your addictive strongholds?

Christ-centered community is a nonnegotiable necessity for true recovery to happen.

>**Leader guide:** After reading the article aloud together, go over the discussion questions. Invite members to journal on their own about Question 4 and write out any fears they might have about being fully known. Then ask them to pray over those fears with God and share some of them with a trusted friend for support and encouragement.

DISCUSSION QUESTIONS

1. How would you define authentic community? What makes such a community different from a crowd of acquaintances?
2. Do you know what wounds need healing in your life (emotional, physical, spiritual)? If not, are you willing to seek help to uncover them?
3. Why is community essential to healing and growth in recovery? What has been your experience in trying to heal and grow apart from community?
4. What does it feel like to belong? To be "known and loved" by someone? What can be scary about this?
5. What makes someone a true friend? How would you define "faithful friendship"?

>**Leader guide:** Allow your time on Question 5 to set up the group exercise of building faithful friendships.

Lesson

GROUP EXERCISE

Making Friends

To recover from addiction, you need friends—faithful friends! A recovery community is a great environment to establish and build such friendships. But what makes these friendships effective? A good friend in recovery will

- listen.
- hold you accountable to your boundaries.
- encourage you when you stumble and help you learn from it.
- point you to God's truth and love.
- share their life with you.
- pray *for* you and *with* you.

Faithful friendship is not merely about recovery. It is about a bond that is mutually beneficial for growing in God's grace and truth. Be careful not to make "friends" that are one-dimensional, only focused on recovery and accountability.

As a group, discuss how you might pursue "faithful friendships" together. This doesn't mean you must "force" friendships with each other. The question is, rather, how can you help each other pursue such friendships, even if they are with others outside the group?

> **Leader guide:** This lesson is all about inviting group members into pursuing "faithful friends" in the environment of "authentic community" for the purpose of healing and growth. This can be scary. But recovery is about doing a lot of scary things:

- Admitting you are out of control and addicted
- Telling someone your full story of brokenness
- Stepping into a group and inviting others to hold you accountable
- Making amends with those you hurt
- Forgiving those who hurt you
- Changing patterns of thought, behavior and boundaries

This is just to name a few! It is important to commend group members for exhibiting great courage as they press into the process of recovery. Remind them that God's grace is sufficient to give them the power and stamina to continue on in the face of fear. Over time, they will realize the benefits of transparent friendships and authentic community.

Wrap up the meeting with prayer and a word of encouragement.

4

Grace to Get Back Up

Main idea: Dealing with failure in recovery

Bible passage: James 5:13-16

GBR article: How grace teaches us to learn from failure

Discussion questions

Group exercise: Practicing true confession

Leader guide: Many who enter recovery have a "fix it" mentality toward the process. They believe that they can enter a support group or see a counselor and, within a very short time, have all the "answers" they need to merrily go on their way. All who embrace such a view quickly discover that this isn't how recovery works. For those who choose to remain, it is important to establish early on the necessity of the disciplines of confession and repentance. Everybody stumbles in recovery. Therefore, everyone must confess failure, not simply from "pre-recovery" missteps but also from "in-recovery" blunders.

    SETUP: Because most addicts learn to isolate and disconnect from real relationships, we tend to think of recovery in such terms. Therefore, we believe that activities like confession and repentance can also be undertaken alone. But "alone" and "recovery" do not equal freedom and transformation. We must accept not only the necessity of confession and repentance as a personal discipline, but also the need for community in practicing such disciplines. Building healthy relationships are an essential core thread throughout a grace-based recovery.

Read the Main idea and Bible passage together.

MAIN IDEA

Recovery is an imperfect journey of stumbling in the right direction. No one travels the road of recovery without falling. No one! This doesn't mean that you are aiming for failure, simply that it is inevitable. But God is more than able to pick you up and give you what you need to take another step. Remember, his grace reminds you that your worth to him is not based on your perfection, but rather on his love.

Jesus is the only one to ever live a perfectly sinless life before God. And because God loves you, the sinless Jesus took the punishment for your sins, dying on your behalf so that your sins might be forgiven. Despite your sinfulness, God considered you worth the life of his perfect Son.

Knowing that God loves you this way, your response to your failures in recovery should lead you to confess them to God, which is followed by repentance. Don't be deceived into thinking that confession was a one-time necessity at the beginning of recovery that never needs to be repeated, or that what you learned in your first step of recovery was all you would ever need to know.

Confession and repentance are core disciplines of recovery. When you stumble, you must confess that to God and to some faithful friends. You must repent of false beliefs about your identity and value to God and any wrong steps you have taken. When you confess and repent, you break the power of darkness, and Jesus, the Light of hope and healing, lifts you up to keep moving forward.

BIBLE PASSAGE

James 5:13-16

Is anyone among you suffering? Let him pray. Is anyone cheerful? Let him sing praise. Is anyone among you sick? Let him call for the elders of the church, and let them pray over him, anointing him with oil in the name of the Lord. And the prayer of faith will save the one who is sick, and the Lord will raise him up. And if he has committed sins, he will be forgiven. Therefore, confess your sins to one another and pray for one another, that you may be healed. The prayer of a righteous person has great power as it is working.

ASK: Why is it important to accept that no one travels the road of recovery without stumbling? How does such a truth make you feel?

ASK: What do you think is the difference between initially sharing your story of brokenness and addiction, and now confessing and repenting as someone in recovery?

ASK: James 5:16 commands us to confess our sins to one another. Why is this important as it pertains to healing? What makes this so difficult in recovery?

Leader guide: This article highlights the one-two punch of confession and repentance when dealing with failures along recovery's journey. Everybody stumbles in recovery. Group members need to understand how to respond to such failures in a way that is instructive and grace-filled so they are encouraged to get back up and keep moving forward.

TRANSITION TO ARTICLE: Whether in recovery or not, everyone stumbles in life. Along life's journey there are missteps and failures. To heal and grow, confession and repentance must occur. But what does this look like and where is this best practiced?

Read the article aloud together.

4

How Grace Teaches Us to Learn from Failure

Failure is inevitable on the pathway to success. This may seem at first like a falsehood. But give yourself a moment to think about it. Name one person who reached any pinnacle of success without being affected by failure. Everyone in life faces failures, mistakes, and detours, whether by their own choices or the choices of others. The universal reality of all mankind is summed up in Romans 3:23, "For all have sinned and fall short of the glory of God."

So how does failure tie to success? Every failure is an opportunity to learn. Thomas Edison, when asked about his many failed attempts at inventing the light bulb, is quoted as saying, "I have not failed. I've just found ten thousand ways that won't work." If failure is viewed as a stop sign, you will cease pursuing "ways that work." But if failure is seen as an opportunity to learn and correct course, you will eventually "see the Light" (pun intended).

The trick to turning failure into success is all in how you respond to your stumbles in recovery. You must develop the one-two punch disciplines of confession and repentance. And you must practice these disciplines in a place we have already introduced: community.

Confession: Uncovering what you did in the dark

Confession is agreeing with the truth, or bringing into the light what is hidden in the dark. It sounds so simple, right? And it is, but that doesn't make it easy to do, especially if you have been compiling secret sins for years. But any real recovery must start—and continue—with confessing what is hidden.

Grace helps you to confess, because it promises that whatever you bring out of the dark won't change how God loves you. It is okay if you do not fully believe this right now. Remember, grace is not easy to receive. But it is still true; your secrets and stumbles do not affect your worth. Embracing this can give you the courage you need to open up and confess every time you fall.

Maybe you have already confessed your secrets to God, and that is good. But you might wonder why you are not free from your addiction. It is not because God is powerless or uncaring. It is because you must also confess to fellow believers. Remember the James passage at the beginning of this lesson? "Confess your sins *to one another* and pray for one another, that you may be healed" (5:16, emphasis mine).

This passage teaches that your sins are not only to be confessed to God (as in 1 John 1:9), but they must also be confessed to one another. Why? So you might be healed, no longer bound by the darkness of secrecy, lies, and shame. You must bring what is hidden out into the open to learn from it, and grace can help you do that.

When you confess, take time to unpack all the steps that led up to the sin and all your reactions afterward. These are clues into your heart. The stumbles in recovery are never only about behavior; they are about motives, thoughts, passions, and wounds. If you simply confess to the behavior without exploring all that surrounded it, you will do little to correct your course the next time you are faced with similar temptations.

This is why it is critical to confess "to one another" and allow trusted friends to help you with your blind spots. Together, and by God's leading, you can discover the areas that need the most attention for making the next best steps forward.

Repentance: Aligning your thoughts and motives with truth

Confession in recovery is only the first step in responding properly to failures. This must be followed up with repentance. To repent is to "change your mind" in the right direction. It is like confession in the sense that you admit to wrong thinking, but it goes further than confession by engaging your will to do something about it. Confession reveals your error and repentance corrects it.

To repent well, it is essential that God's Word, the Bible, be your ultimate source for truth and wisdom. Friends are good. Counselors are helpful. Even pastors have their strategic place in your recovery. But none are a substitute for the eternal, inerrant Word of God. You must discipline yourself to "change your mind" toward the truth of Scripture. This is the true discipline of repentance.

Grace-based recovery is a journey of ever-growing success. If you want to enjoy such success, you must confess and repent when you stumble. Here is the basic progression of this confession-repentance process:

1. You stumble in some way.
2. You confess what you did to God and trusted friends.
3. You unpack the details surrounding the stumble to uncover false beliefs, wrong motives, and other errors in thinking or decision-making.
4. You repent of any untruths in thinking and replace them with the truths of God's Word.
5. You construct a plan with trusted friends for a better response to similar temptations down the road.
6. You pray and keep pressing on.

Though failure is inevitable along the road of recovery, it doesn't need to define the outcome of your journey. Devote yourself to confession and repentance so that you can learn from your mistakes and enjoy the long-term success of a grace-based recovery.

> **Leader guide:** After reading the article together, go over the discussion questions. Invite members to spend some time on their own with Question 3 and pray for their fellow group members during the week ahead.

DISCUSSION QUESTIONS

1. What is the difference between confession and repentance? How do these differences complement each other?
2. Why are both confession and repentance necessary when responding to failure in recovery? Why couldn't you simply respond with confession *or* repentance?
3. James 5:16 instructs us to "pray for one another" in addition to confessing our sins to one another. Why is this additional instruction important? What do you think such prayer looks like?
4. Why is it important to unpack what happened before and after your sinful behavior and not just the behavior itself?
5. How can you better adopt a mindset of learning from your mistakes?

> **Leader guide:** Allow your time on Question 4 to set up the group exercise of practicing true confession.

4

Practicing True Confession

Let's not pretend that confession and repentance are easy disciplines to practice. But you wouldn't have gotten this far in this study if you hadn't already done some hard things in recovery. Admitting you need help is a hard thing to do, and here you are. So, just because something is hard to do doesn't mean that it isn't the right thing to do. Much of recovery is learning to do hard things that are good for you. Confessing when you mess up is good to do. Repenting and turning your mind toward truth is good to do.

As a group, let's practice true confession and repentance. And remember, this is a No Shame Zone, so everyone is here to help and support each other toward success!

Everyone, think of one instance of failure in your past that you can confess (even if it has been confessed before; this is about practice). But rather than just confess the behavior, think about the factors that led up to it and the reactions you had afterward. Make this part of the confession too.

- What triggered you?
- Where did your thoughts go?
- What emotions did you feel?
- Can you connect those emotions to anything in your past? Your childhood?
- What did you feel afterward?
- What did you think afterward?
- What did you do afterward?

As you confess these experiences, take note of any lies, false beliefs, wounds, misdirected motives, etc. that come out. These are the points at which repentance will be necessary, and the points where correction for future encounters can be made.

Spend time praying for each other and encouraging each other toward greater honesty and openness.

> **Leader guide:** This lesson is critical for understanding the reality of stumbling along the path of recovery and realizing that such failures are opportunities to learn rather than quit. The key disciplines that must be practiced to do this well are confession and repentance, before God and trusted friends.
>
> Encourage members that failure is not fatal if responded to properly. They can succeed in recovery by God's grace, which offers them a "do over" for every misstep. Stress the need for building and maintaining strong, faithful friendships for this kind of openness and accountability.
>
> Wrap up the meeting with prayer and a word of encouragement.

Lesson

5

Grace to Persevere

Main idea: Embracing faithfulness

Bible passage: James 1:22-25; Proverbs 27:17

GBR article: Keep on keeping on

Discussion questions

Group exercise: Daily disciplines that affect freedom

Leader guide: Successful recovery results from retraining in thoughts, motives, and behavior over a long period of time. Grace-based recovery is about understanding and applying the truth regarding one's identity in Christ on a more consistent basis. This takes lots of time and faithful perseverance. Knowing what to do is only the first step. Practicing such knowledge daily over time is what leads to real transformation and freedom.

SETUP: This lesson is all about faithful perseverance. It invites you to embark on personal and relational disciplines that lead to better health and contentment. The key element in this lesson is the necessity to practice what one already knows. For most in recovery, the real issue is not ignorance (not knowing the right thing to do), but rather practice (actually doing the right thing). The James 1 passage about being "doers of the word" is key throughout the lesson.

Read the Main idea and Bible passage together.

MAIN IDEA

Grace-based recovery is not a short journey. Recovery is a process and the process takes time—but not *just* time. Recovery is an active process of embarking on entirely new ways to think, relate, and act. This requires faithful endurance on your part to stick with this process through all its peaks and valleys. You must learn to persevere if you expect to be set free from addictive strongholds.

BIBLE PASSAGE

James 1:22-25

> But be doers of the word, and not hearers only, deceiving your-selves. For if anyone is a hearer of the word and not a doer, he is like a man who looks intently at his natural face in a mirror. For he looks at himself and goes away and at once forgets what he was like. But the one who looks into the perfect law, the law of liberty, and perseveres, being no hearer who forgets but a doer who acts, he will be blessed in his doing.

Proverbs 27:17

> Iron sharpens iron,
>   and one man sharpens another.

ASK: Why do you believe recovery takes such a long time? Why is this good?

ASK: What is the difference between "academic" knowledge and "application" knowledge? What difference do you think this makes in recovery?

ASK: How would you define or describe perseverance?

Leader guide: There are two key kinds of "knowing" addressed in this article: (1) intellectual knowledge, and (2) practical knowledge. It is important that group members be pushed to pursue the latter without ignoring the former. But be assured that no real recovery occurs by virtue of intellectual knowledge alone. Such knowledge without application will only result in a really smart addict!

TRANSITION TO ARTICLE: This week's article is about persistence in the daily practices of a life of freedom and sobriety. Such a life does not happen magically. God's grace is not a magic wand that eliminates our responsibility to apply that grace to our will and actions. God expects the gift of his grace to be unwrapped and applied to every area of our lives. We'll spend time unpacking what this can look like personally and relationally in recovery.

Read the article aloud together.

Keep on Keeping On

Most recovery programs, as we've stated in earlier lessons, focus solely (or at least primarily) on modifying or controlling behavior. But that is not what recovery really needs to be about. That is a shallow and short-term vision. Grace-based recovery calls you to be faithful in recovery, in relationships, in life.

Faithfulness is about remaining true to a person, a cause, or a belief. This is a tall order for an addict, because addiction simply follows wherever the urges might lead. There is no loyalty or fidelity in addiction. If a "better offer" comes along, the addicted person lunges toward it without any thought of the consequences.

Recovery is good because it leads to sanity and sobriety. It helps you step off the "merry-go-round" of craziness that only spins faster and faster the longer you ride it. In recovery you are finally able to stop long enough to clear your head, find your bearings, and focus on a pathway to real change and health.

It is incredibly important that you learn to be faithful in the process of recovery. This requires saying no to urges you have always allowed, committing to healthy outlets for dealing with temptation, and keeping your word. To be faithful is to embrace recovery and be loyal to the process, especially when you are tempted to step off the path.

However, when you do step off the path, as someone who is growing in faithfulness, you will more quickly return to your recovery. By grace, your stumbling can never disqualify you from the journey. Faithfulness is not about never failing, but rather about always eventually returning to your commitment to recovery when you do fall.

FAITHFULNESS: DOING THE RIGHT THING OVER AND OVER AGAIN

God's Word reminds us that it isn't enough to just know the truth. God expects us to "do" the truth. To put this in recovery language, it isn't enough to just know what freedom and sobriety are; you must do what free and sober people do. Grace-based recovery means becoming acquainted experientially with your true identity in Christ as a free, faithful child of God. This isn't a process of just gaining more head knowledge. It's time to put what you already know into practice.

I would be shocked if you told me that you didn't know the right thing to do in relationship to your particular addictive struggle. In other words, your problem is not ignorance. You know the difference between right and wrong, between sober and addicted. You know where that line is because you have crossed it many times. So don't pretend that your struggle is with knowledge. It isn't! Your struggle is with practice. You struggle with applying your will, by God's grace, to do the right thing. (It's okay; this is the basic struggle for every human being!)

I'm not saying that you can't grow in your knowledge of what is right. We can all benefit from a deeper knowledge of truth. But there are limits to knowledge. And the kind of "knowing" that an addict needs is rarely intellectual. An addict needs to know the truth the way a carpenter knows his hammer. A carpenter doesn't carry around a picture of a hammer, pull it out at his jobsite, and explain how it works to the customer. No, he carries an *actual* hammer and "knows" it by repeatedly swinging it to complete the job. He may not hit the nail every time, but he has swung it enough to know how it operates in action, not just in theory.

You, too, will need to pick up the "hammer" of recovery and get to swinging it. I know you won't hit the nail every time (maybe for a long time), but it's the only way you can "do" recovery. This hammer of recovery contains all the basic principles of a life of integrity (confession, repentance, self-awareness, faith, community, service). As you grow in your faithful practice of grace-based recovery, your skill in each area will improve. Not because you know *about* such principles, but rather because you are *practicing* such principles in your daily life. You must swing the hammer every day.

PERSISTENCE WILL PAY OFF— EVENTUALLY

Grace-based recovery leads you on a *long* journey, not because recovery is about seeing how much you can suffer, but because real transformation takes a long time. No one gets well overnight. This means that persistence is key to long-term change.

Proverbs 27:17 (one of this lesson's Bible passages) is often used as the theme verse for men's ministries. It paints a great picture of iron being sharpened into useful tools or weapons. But the poetic nature of the verse may cause one to miss the grueling reality it portrays.

Imagine that you held two iron rods in your hands. Each is eighteen inches long and rounded. You need to put a sharp edge on both rods but can only use the other rod to do so. What does this picture look like now? Poetic? Fast? Easy?

You will actually have quite a long process ahead of you. You must press the rods into each other—hard! This will create pressure, heat, friction, and even sparks when the imperfections in each rod strike against the other. All of sudden you realize that this is no easy, fast process. In order to create sharp rods, you must be persistent.

The same is true of becoming a "sharp" man or woman of sobriety, no longer bound to your addictive ways. You must press into others on the journey, expecting friction, pressure, and sparks that fly. But you must not give up on the process! If at any point you stop pressing in, you both will suffer.

If you chose to stop striking those iron rods against each other, what likelihood is there that a sharp edge would appear on either rod? None! You must continue applying pressure in order to sharpen the rods. You must also continue pressing into other "rods" (people) in your recovery if you (and they) are to become sharp and useful.

Grace allows us the time we need to persist in recovery. Pressure, friction, heat, and sparks are very unpleasant on the journey, even if we know what the intended result is meant to be. When you grow weary and decide to coast, grace reminds you of your value, and the value of those on the journey with you. It invites you to keep pressing in even though you are tired.

Giving up only results in your addiction getting worse. Keep pressing on in recovery and you will become a powerful weapon for good, not only in your life but in the lives of those around you.

> **Leader guide:** After reading the article aloud, go over the discussion questions. Encourage members to unpack Questions 2-3 even further on their own.

DISCUSSION QUESTIONS

1. What makes quitting recovery seem so attractive at times? How can you better resist such temptations?
2. In what areas do you struggle most in being faithful? What is one thing you could do this week to improve in those areas?
3. How can you better apply your knowledge of recovery to your daily practices to combat temptation and grow in grace and truth?
4. Why does "giving up only result in getting worse"?
5. In what areas of your recovery are you not "swinging the hammer"? What will you do this week to sharpen your focus and persist in "doing" recovery?

Leader guide: Lots of people in recovery like to debate ideas. They question the validity or value of various methods and strategies. It can all sound very intelligent. But remind yourself that they are still addicted and in need of recovery. That should tell you that their "smarts" alone have not set them free! Gently redirect any "debaters" back to the central theme of this lesson: daily practice of the truth leads to transformation.

Allow your time on Question 5 to set up the group exercise of daily disciplines that affect freedom.

5

**GROUP
EXERCISE**

Daily Disciplines That Affect Freedom

This lesson's article lists six principles that make up the "hammer" of recovery you are to "work out" daily: confession, repentance, self-awareness, faith, community, service. This group exercise will help you start outlining specific actions you can take to grow your skill in these areas.

Take a piece of paper or a journal and write down the six principles listed. For each principle, share something specific that you could do to grow in that area. For example, for "faith" you could

- read your Bible every day before going to work.
- pray (alone, with your spouse, with a friend, at a prayer meeting, etc.).
- attend a Bible study in your church or community.
- regularly attend worship at a local church.

Share your ideas with each other and encourage accountability for pursuing at least one specific area in the coming week. Be careful not to add too many things to your list. Pursue faithfulness in a few specific disciplines and increase your commitments gradually. It is through faithfulness and perseverance that one grows "sharp" in God's kingdom.

> **Leader guide:** The faithful, persistent practice of God's Word leads to freedom, joy, and usefulness in his kingdom. Encourage growth in small, daily practices.
>
> Wrap up the meeting with prayer and a word of encouragement.

Lesson

6

Grace to Forgive

Main idea: The two sides of forgiveness

Bible passage: Colossians 3:12-13

GBR article: The grace to make amends

Discussion questions

Group exercise: Living out the Golden Rule

Leader guide: This lesson may be one of the most important—and difficult. An unwillingness to forgive is a cancer that destroys whoever harbors it. Many in recovery are suffering terribly because of past wounds. They suffer twice as much when they do not forgive. This is a delicate area to address. Be aware of your limitations as a group facilitator and freely recommend professional counseling to those who are especially triggered by this lesson.

SETUP: No single lesson on recovery can comprehensively address the issue of forgiveness. So this is very much a "fly over" lesson intended to help group members understand the key elements of forgiveness as they pertain to the recovery journey. It is imperative that forgiveness be addressed in the context of God's Word and his definitions.

Read the Main idea and Bible passage together.

MAIN IDEA

Sin hurts people. I could have said "addiction hurts people" and that would have been true too. But the engine of addiction is sin. It is a disease that has infected every human being since Adam and Eve. And sin hurts people. It hurts the offended as well as the offender. Sin causes wounds. And wounds need healing if true recovery is going to happen.

The cure for sin's wounds is not psychology, or psychiatry, or sincere promises. The cure is forgiveness, but not the world's kind of forgiveness that comes with all kinds of strings attached. The forgiveness that heals sin's wounds can only originate from God. This is why grace-based recovery is so important. Apart from the forgiveness we are given by God, there is no hope for real freedom or change or life. This is the forgiveness you must receive if you want real transformation.

BIBLE PASSAGE

Colossians 3:12-13

> Put on then, as God's chosen ones, holy and beloved, compassionate hearts, kindness, humility, meekness, and patience, bearing with one another and, if one has a complaint against another, forgiving each other; as the Lord has forgiven you, so you also must forgive.

ASK: What does it mean to forgive? Why is this important to the recovery process?

ASK: What distinguishes God's forgiveness from the world's "forgiveness"?

ASK: How has sin hurt you? How has your sin hurt others?

Leader guide: Forgiveness is not optional in recovery. You cannot stand before God with an unforgiving spirit toward someone and offer an acceptable excuse for it. You must forgive. But forgiveness need not be immediate following the offense.

There must be time to grieve and process the damage. Then, by God's grace, the decision to forgive must be made and carried out.

Again, be sensitive to the nature of this topic. Every person in recovery has wounds from their past. Some are very deep and painful. This is a wonderful opportunity to practice grace-based recovery by creating a safe enough place for hurts to be uncovered.

TRANSITION TO ARTICLE: Grace-based recovery establishes that our ability to forgive others is grounded in our first receiving God's forgiveness for our sins. If we have not experienced God's forgiveness ourselves, we have no real way forward in trying to forgive others. We cannot offer to others what we do not possess ourselves.

Forgiveness takes time. While there may be watershed moments of "big" forgiving, past offenses have a way of popping back up in our minds. It's important to remember that forgiveness is an ongoing decision to not hold our offender's guilt against him. We leave room for God's justice through our trust in him.

Read the article aloud together.

Lesson

6

ARTICLE

The Grace to Make Amends

Every addict has been hurt by someone else, and every addict has also hurt someone they love. Since addicts learn to cope with pain through abusive means (drugs, alcohol, cutting, porn, illicit sex, etc.), they tend to transmit the pain they suffered onto others. Therefore, if real change is going to occur, forgiveness is essential.

Remember Joe? Let's check back with him now.

> "Joe, so good to see you back at group this week. And thanks for sharing about some of your really tough childhood. I'm so sorry your neighbor took advantage of you like that. That must have been really painful and confusing."
>
> "It was. For years I felt such debilitating shame about the whole thing. I felt like I was to blame, but I also didn't know what I could have done about it. I mean, he was six years older than I was and I never felt like I had a choice. Over time, I hated myself as much as I hated him. I still hate him. I know I'm supposed to forgive him for what he did, but I don't know how to let go of my anger and hate."
>
> "What if I told you that you didn't need to let go of it right now? How would that make you feel?"
>
> "Good, I guess. But at the same time I can't stand carrying around all this hatred. I'm just such an angry person and I seem

to be able to trace it all back to him. I mean, I like the idea of not putting so much pressure on myself to forgive, but I'm tired of carrying the hate."

"Why don't we work on your heart first? Then we can deal with thinking about forgiving your neighbor. You might find that forgiveness will seem more palatable when you start gaining a new view of yourself. When you begin to see yourself as God sees you, through the lens of love, you might feel more of a freedom to offer your neighbor the forgiveness he doesn't deserve."

"That's a relief. It seems like every Christian I've talked to has just added to the pressure I already feel to forgive that jerk, but I just don't want to. I would like to do what you're saying and see if I could start to see myself differently. Because right now I can only see myself as a damaged scumbag."

Forgiveness is a process, a painful and difficult one. There is agony in forgiveness because it requires forgivers to choose *not* to punish the one who offended them. Joe's neighbor deserved to be punished for what he did—severely! That's why Joe's process of forgiveness wasn't easy. He had to decide if he wanted to release his neighbor from the penalty he deserved. That is no easy decision.

Too often in recovery, well-meaning people give bad advice regarding forgiveness. Some handle it too lightly and make it an optional part of recovery. But a failure to forgive always results in further bondage to one's abuser. Others handle forgiveness too rigidly, demanding that this tough decision be made immediately, without regard for the addict's deep wounds. Neither way is helpful.

Grace offers another avenue for forgiveness, a way that takes into account the pain suffered and the need for a new perspective on it, a new vantage point. Most addicts have been reeling from the pain of their wounds for years, building up decades of resentment and hatred toward their abusers.

Over time, addicts develop intense shame and then, as a result of their own addiction, they end up hurting others. This means that their vantage point is that of a bitter, angry victim. On some level, they probably feel like they deserve exactly what their abusers deserve. And in one respect (as sinful human beings who have rebelled against their Creator) they are right. But this blinds addicts from seeing clearly what their wounds were all about: someone else's brokenness got dumped into their life.

Joe wasn't to blame for what his neighbor did to him, even if Joe later went along with it. That was his neighbor's brokenness, not Joe's. But twenty-five years later, when Joe was ready to work on recovery from his own addiction, he couldn't see the abuse so clearly. He blamed himself, hated himself, and cursed himself, all for what his neighbor did to him.

Grace pulls back the curtain that hides the little kid inside you. It shows you that what happened to that kid was not your fault. It wasn't right or good, but it wasn't your fault. This allows you to begin healing from the wounds, so that you can eventually take the next step toward forgiveness.

It is likely that when you start seeing how someone else's brokenness was forced into your life, you will become even angrier. Not necessarily a vengeful kind of anger, but more like a righteous anger. You may weep over your child self who was unable to fight off the abuser. You may feel deep pain that in some ways hurts even more than the original abuse did. This is normal. Yet this can be healing when you release this pain to God and entrust justice to his timetable and methods.

When you gain this new view of your past wounds and have felt a cleansing of your soul through grieving your losses,[1] you will be in a much better place to work on forgiveness. Grieving alone cannot fully release you from your past; you must forgive. This is where grace comes in.

> Put on then, as God's chosen ones, holy and beloved, compassionate hearts, kindness, humility, meekness, and patience,

---

1. Professional counseling can be helpful when dealing with past abuse and wounds. For help finding a counselor, visit AACC.net or call 1-800-A-FAMILY.

bearing with one another and, if one has a complaint against another, forgiving each other; **as the Lord has forgiven you, so you also must forgive**. (Colossians 3:12-13, emphasis mine)

The best way to understand how to forgive someone who hurt you is to understand how God has forgiven you. You have offended God with your sin (me too; see Romans 6:23). You deserve to be punished for your sins (me too; see Romans 6:23 again). But God instead chooses to forgive (Romans 3:21-24; Ephesians 1:7; Colossians 2:13-15; 1 John 1:9). He chooses the law of love, to pay the price you owed (death) to give you a gift you did not deserve (eternal life). As you meditate on that truth and embrace it deep in your soul, your heart will have the strength, security, and freedom to begin to soften toward those who hurt you.

Keep in mind, though, that forgiveness is a choice. Your feelings may not coincide with what you know you must do. This does not mean that feelings don't matter when it comes to forgiveness; only that they are not the determining factor in choosing to forgive those who have wronged you.

Forgiveness doesn't always mean that there will be a restoration of relationships, nor should it. Some people are unhealthy and dangerous. Forgiveness is simply one of the means by which you will be released from the shackles of anger, fear, and shame that bind you to your past wounds. And God's grace is what will carry you through as you ask him for his help, wisdom and strength to walk this road.

WHAT ABOUT THE OTHER SIDE OF FORGIVENESS?

Recovery will teach you two things about wounds: (1) you have been hurt, and (2) you have hurt others. There is no escaping the truth that your addictive patterns have hurt someone else. While you may not have hurt someone as severely as Joe's neighbor hurt him, your self-centered behaviors have offended someone who loves you. This is a wound that needs healing.

You cannot force someone to forgive you, but you can seek to make amends through humble confession and genuine remorse. And even if they choose to withhold forgiveness from you, God sees your heart and promises to honor those who honor him. Seek a clear conscience and to be at peace with everyone. Recovery is messy, but try to make things as right as you possibly can. God will help you.

> **Leader guide:** After reading the article, go over the discussion questions. As you do, be aware of anyone becoming "closed off." This can be a sign that this issue is hitting very hard and the person might need outside professional help. Be gentle and inviting to see if they will participate, but don't push too hard.
>
> Encourage members to do Question 4 on their own. It is amazing how God can use that simple act to open up hearts and melt away shame. Allow your time on Questions 2-3 to set up the group exercise of living out the Golden Rule

DISCUSSION QUESTIONS

1. How does it make you feel to know that forgiveness is essential to the recovery process?
2. Is there anyone in your past that you have not forgiven? Anyone in your present? What will you do to begin unpacking that pain?
3. Who have you hurt by your selfish actions? What will you do to express sorrow and repentance?
4. Spend time journaling about how God has forgiven you. Worship and praise him for his grace and kindness toward you.
5. Is anything blocking you from receiving and embracing the forgiveness of God? The forgiveness of others? How can you begin to remove that blockage so you can experience the fullness of forgiveness?

Lesson

6

**GROUP
EXERCISE**

Living Out
the Golden Rule

Did you know that the Golden Rule is from the Bible? It is. Luke 6:31 says, "And as you wish that others would do to you, do so to them." Why are we bringing this up for a group exercise on the topic of forgiveness? Because the Golden Rule is a great way to get ahead of the whole forgiveness issue. When you treat others with empathy, it is very hard to sin against them. Think of it as preempting the need to ask for forgiveness.

But we do need to address the actual practice of forgiveness. As a group, discuss the following two questions and any roadblocks preventing you from taking action:

- Who do you need to forgive?
- Who do you need to make amends with?

Leader guide: If anyone needs outside professional help for dealing with issues of forgiveness and shame, direct them to AACC.net.

Wrap up the meeting with prayer and a word of encouragement.

Lesson

7

Grace to Grow Up

Main idea: Growing in body, soul, and spirit—for a greater purpose

Bible passages: 1 Corinthians 13:11; Ephesians 2:8-10

GBR article: The skill (and art) of growing up

Discussion questions

Group exercise: How to put away childish ways

Leader guide: No one likes to admit that they are immature. Those in recovery often prefer to see themselves as victims. This isn't entirely untrue, but it doesn't paint the full picture. What has been done to you never excuses the decisions you choose now. And every addict makes poor decisions. The issue of "growing up" must be addressed. But as with everything else in grace-based recovery, this needs to be done with gentleness and respect. The best way to lead out on difficult topics is to use yourself as the test subject whenever possible. This can break the ice for others to admit their struggles with immaturity and living for a greater purpose.

SETUP: Possibly the best way to set up this lesson would be to share a personal story of immaturity or poor decision-making on your part. It doesn't even need to be directly related to recovery, simply a story that shows that everyone does stupid stuff at some point. Then leverage this story to show the need for correction in your thinking and decision-making for the future, because if you stay stuck in your immaturity, you will never fulfill the purpose for which God made you.

Read the Main idea and Bible passages together.

MAIN IDEA

Addiction breeds immaturity. Don't take this too personally! No one who gets addicted to anything did so exclusively as an adult. In other words, the roots of addiction always form in childhood. Therefore, once any addictive pattern takes hold, it will water those roots of childish thought and reasoning—the idea that life is all about me.

Grace-based recovery, on the other hand, teaches that life is a gift from God. In order to enjoy it properly, you must grow in humility, wisdom, and service. This, essentially, is the exact opposite of childishness. But be warned. Recovery is actually more about what you *pursue* than what you *avoid*. Learn to move toward what is right and you will simultaneously be moving away from what is wrong.

BIBLE PASSAGES

1 Corinthians 13:11

When I was a child, I spoke like a child, I thought like a child, I reasoned like a child. When I became a man, I gave up childish ways.

Ephesians 2:8-10

For by grace you have been saved through faith. And this is not your own doing; it is the gift of God, not a result of works, so that no one may boast. For we are his workmanship, created in Christ Jesus for good works, which God prepared beforehand, that we should walk in them.

ASK: What is the difference between childish and childlike? Why does this matter when discussing "growing up" in recovery? (Hint: Childish has to do with immature thinking, while childlike has to do with innocence and trust in God.)

ASK: Describe key distinctions between child thinking and adult thinking.

ASK: Why is growth in character more about what you are pursuing than what you are avoiding? (Hint: Godliness has to do with faithful obedience—seeking God's kingdom and his righteousness. Merely avoiding unrighteousness is only the first basic step toward godly maturity.)

TRANSITION TO ARTICLE: Success in recovery is largely born out of growing in wisdom. And wisdom is the right application of knowledge. Wisdom is kind of a grownup thing. Children are self-absorbed. Mature adults are sacrificial. Children follow their urges. Mature adults choose what's right despite their urges. Children complain when they don't get their way. Mature adults acknowledge that life doesn't revolve around them.

We need reminders in recovery that the paradigm of self-centeredness must shift if transformation is to occur. This article will help us ponder this shift and pursue a far greater purpose than self-gratification.

Let's read the article aloud together.

ARTICLE

The Skill (and Art) of Growing Up

Some recovery programs convey an unspoken mandate: you must be "in recovery" for the rest of your life. In other words, if you are not in group or in some other sort of program to manage your addiction, you will not make it. But true recovery is more than simply not acting out. True recovery is about growth in body, soul, and spirit.

Recovery reveals your heart, the good and the bad. You see where you are doing well and you see what needs improvement. There is a lot of self-awareness that comes when you are seriously engaged in recovery.

As these parts of your being are revealed, you start to realize that recovery is about a lot more than your acting-out behaviors. In fact, you start to wonder if this recovery thing is actually about your entire life being transformed. *It is!* From your work to how you talk to managing finances to building relationships to thoughts and motives, recovery is about total transformation.

To say that the vision for your life and future is simply to stop acting out is an incredibly weak vision. How uninspiring! To *not* act out? What kind of a vision is *not* doing something? And what direction would you go next if you succeeded in not acting out? What would you be striving *for* at that point?

Here is a different vision for recovery—a lasting and inspiring vision: to grow in your faith in Christ and service to others. You were made to be whole, fully alive, and thriving in Christ, and to fulfill a purpose that encompasses your mind, body, soul, and spirit. You were not made to continue spiraling downward in a self-destructive pattern of addiction. Do you want to be free? Get on a mission of growth, not merely a mission of "not acting out"!

Grace helps you grow as a person because grace reveals your true identity.

> For by grace you have been saved through faith. And this is not your own doing; it is the gift of God, not a result of works, so that no one may boast. For we are his workmanship, created in Christ Jesus for good works, which God prepared beforehand, that we should walk in them. (Ephesians 2:8-10)

You are the workmanship of God, created for good works. You were made to fulfill a purpose that is God-sized. Recovery that focuses on "not doing" is counter to who you were made to be. You have been given a purpose that is so big that you could not fulfill it, if it were not for God's grace. But because of his grace, you can! Beware, though, of the resistance you will face to this truth.

Shame is often a huge stumbling block to those in recovery. It is behind the lies that cause you to believe you are worthless as a result of your selfish, addictive actions. It attacks your true identity and calls into question whether anyone (even God) could really love and accept you. It leads you away from who you were made to be. Shame says that you are not worth recovery.

Grace, however, leads you on a different path, one that reminds you that your value is not tied to your failures, and your identity is not based on what you do (or don't do). Grace invites you on a journey of growth, fully aware that you will stumble along the way. But just because you fall, that doesn't mean you cannot get up and press on to uncover the new you.

Embrace a vision of recovery that encompasses your whole being. If you only focus on the spiritual, your emotional and physical self will suffer. If you only focus on your emotional issues, your body and spirit will suffer. If you only focus on the physical (i.e. behavior), your emotional and spiritual selves will languish. You are body, soul, and spirit, so your recovery needs to be about growth in all these areas.

Start with simple things, like your eating and sleeping habits. Make sure you are getting good rest and regular exercise. You don't have to be extreme, but recovery is hard enough without adding to it the trouble that comes from lack of sleep and poor nutrition.

Personal growth is a lifelong venture, not merely a "part" of recovery. Make it your mission to pursue personal growth at every stage of life. You are never too old to keep growing and maturing. And grace allows for all the stumbles that come with such a mission.

No one does recovery perfectly, but for those who commit to growth no matter what it takes, theirs is a new life of incredible fulfillment and joy. And out of such a life come blessings of immeasurable value that can then be poured out on everyone they touch.

FROM CHILD TO ADULT: PUTTING AWAY CHILDISH WAYS

There is a vast difference between child*like* and child*ish*. One leads to faith that can toss mountains into the sea, and the other leaves broken lives and dreams in its wake. God wants to transform your heart to be a giver rather than taker, a lover rather than luster, a servant rather than a master. But he will not force such change on your heart. You must want it.

> When Jesus saw him lying there and knew that he had already been there a long time, he said to him, "Do you want to be healed?" (John 5:6)

In recovery, you will recognize a lot of things about yourself that aren't pretty. You will see that you are broken. You will see that you are selfish. You will see anger, fear, entitlement, pride, and many other characteristics that reveal an adult-sized toddler living deep inside you, who wants his toys and will throw a fit if he doesn't get them. This is the childish you. Grace-based recovery is inviting this "you" to grow up.

Childish you will not be happy during this process. Childish you will whine, scream, stomp around, and demand. But the new you must not give in. The new you must choose to "give up childish ways" in order to grow up to maturity. Be patient with yourself in this process. Extend grace to yourself. Ask God for wisdom and faith to choose what is best and right over what is merely convenient. Commit to growing up and do not allow childish you to reign any longer. The tyranny of childish ways must be ended!

> **Leader guide:** No one likes having their childishness pointed out. So don't point it out. Let the members admit it. They have to discover it for there to be any change in them. You can't force growing up in anyone else. Therefore, allow your time in the discussion questions to draw people out. Encourage confession of immaturity, but don't try to force it from anyone. Ask the Holy Spirit to fall heavy on your group during this lesson. He knows best how to draw out his kids and lead them forward.
>
> **Leader guide:** Go over the discussion questions.

DISCUSSION QUESTIONS

1. In what ways are you still thinking and acting in "childish ways"? How will you "give up" such ways and seek to mature?
2. You were "created in Christ Jesus for good works" (Ephesians 2:10). How does this change your perspective on your recovery journey?
3. Why is "don't act out" a weak vision for recovery?
4. How can you combat the shame and lies that want to keep you stuck in addiction?

5. What are several ways you can focus on growth in body, soul, and spirit in the coming week?

> **Leader guide:** Spend some time talking about the "don't act out" vision and why it doesn't work. Point members back to Ephesians 2:10 and the idea that God has made them for a purpose, for good works that he prepared for them to do. Ask them if this kind of God-sized purpose is something that can happen through self-centered, childish ways. Ask them what is at stake from God's perspective if they never "give up" their childish ways.
>
> Allow your time on Question 5 to set up the group exercise.

Lesson

7

GROUP
EXERCISE

How to Put Away Childish Ways

The article in this lesson emphasized the importance of growing in body, soul, and spirit, and giving up childish ways. You might be thinking, *Well, that sounds good, but as one who has lived in such childish ways, how do I recognize my childishness and then give up such ways?* This exercise will help you pursue healthy growth in body, soul, and spirit and, in doing so, begin to expose areas of childish thinking and behaving.

Rank how healthy you believe you are in the following areas (1=weak, 5=strong)

> Physical health
> Emotional health
> Spiritual health
> Relational health

Name one thing you have done in the past week to improve your health in any of these areas.

_____

List as many things as you can that you have done in the past week from pure motives to serve others at your own expense.

List as many things as you can that you have done in the past week from impure motives to serve yourself at someone else's expense.

Discuss these answers with the group and help each other see where your key growth points might be for "giving up childish ways" in favor of more mature, selfless living.

For homework, write down your plan for growth in the areas above and seek accountability from other group members to stick with your plan.

> **Leader guide:** This lesson might feel overwhelming to some members. Remind them of what you discussed in Lesson 5 about faithful perseverance. Maturity doesn't happen overnight. Encourage them to simply focus on one or two areas in the coming weeks where they will seek greater maturity, for the purpose of engaging in the good works God has prepared for them to do. Little steps in the right direction over time will lead them to maturity and fulfilled purpose.
>
> Wrap up the meeting with prayer and a word of encouragement.

8

Grace to Love Well

Main Idea: Love is the goal (grace is to be given away)

Bible passages: John 15:12-14; 1 Peter 4:8

GBR article: The gift worth giving away

Discussion questions

Group exercise: Speaking blessing over others

Leader guide: Love is our highest calling. Therefore, true recovery must point us to love. This can be a hard connection for some in recovery to make. But this lesson will hopefully help to make that connection.

SETUP: Most people in recovery are not good at building healthy relationships. Addiction leads to isolation and loneliness because it maintains a rigid self-focus. Love is the antidote to this self-centered paradigm of addiction. You can know that you are "succeeding" in recovery when you find yourself giving away all you have learned and gained to others in need of similar help. You want to fan this flame of loving service!

Read the Main idea and Bible passages together.

MAIN IDEA

Grace-based recovery is ultimately about building healthy relationships with God and others. Recovery's primary goal cannot merely be modifying your behavior. The essence of life is not found in behavior; it is found in relationships. Therefore, the goal of true recovery is to love well, not just behave well. Loving God and loving others from a pure heart is the foundation of a life free from the bondage of addiction.

As a result of grace-based recovery, a shift in the focus of your heart from self to others must take place. If you reach the one-year anniversary of your start date of recovery and you still believe that the goal is all about you and your sobriety, you have sadly missed the point. But it's never too late to set your sights on love and to allow the grace and truth of God to transform your heart for the next leg of the journey.

BIBLE PASSAGES

John 15:12-14

"This is my commandment, that you love one another as I have loved you. Greater love has no one than this, that someone lay down his life for his friends. You are my friends if you do what I command you."

1 Peter 4:8

Above all, keep loving one another earnestly, since love covers a multitude of sins.

ASK: What is the connection between recovery and healthy relationships? Why are healthy relationships a good barometer of success in recovery?

ASK: Jesus commands that we love others the way he has loved us. In what ways has Jesus loved you? How can you love others in the same way?

ASK: What makes loving others a better goal in recovery than simply not acting out?

Leader guide: This week's article is about growing in compassion through grace-based recovery, and about giving away what you learn to others. This is very unnatural for someone who has been bound up in addiction. Someone may say that they understand what it means to give, but their lifestyle says otherwise. Heart change requires patience and persistence. It also requires the movement of the Holy Spirit. Invite members to ask God to soften their hearts and to be open to his leading as he seeks to transform them from takers to givers.

TRANSITION TO ARTICLE: In some ways, addicts become hoarders. They are so accustomed to taking that the idea of giving is foreign. It hurts. This article points out the need for the heart to change. Therefore, giving away your grace-based recovery is not a cold, calculated decision you make along the way. It is the result of a heart softening toward God, with the "melt-off" spilling out onto others. The heart must change. Compassion must grow. Love must reign.

Let's read the article aloud together.

Lesson

8

ARTICLE

The Gift Worth Giving Away

You were made to be a great lover, not a great luster.

—Stephen Cervantes, HopeCounseling.com

Addiction teaches you to be a taker, someone who does not care about anyone, including yourself. You learn to lie, steal, cheat, abuse, manipulate, and isolate. Life becomes a never-ending pursuit of self-absorbed rituals, all for the momentary pleasure of highs that kill your body, soul, and spirit. But you were made for so much more.

The human heart was made by God to love and be loved. First John 4:9-11 speaks to this truth.

> In this the love of God was made manifest among us, that God sent his only Son into the world, so that we might live through him. In this is love, not that we have loved God but that he loved us and sent his Son to be the propitiation for our sins. Beloved, if God so loved us, we also ought to love one another.

At the core of who you are is a need to be fully known and fully loved. Grace-based recovery reveals your purpose: You were made for love.

Love is fundamentally the opposite of addiction. There is no love in addiction. Love is kind, patient, not self-seeking. Addiction is none of that! Love is all about grace, not reaching out and caring because it wants something in return. Love gives and gives and gives. Love is at the heart of God's grace.

In grace-based recovery, you begin to see that your true worth is not based on your performance. You take steps toward cleaning up and discover the difficulty of the task, all the many things that must change for you to experience peace and health. But along this path you will discover the most important thing: the love of God and the fellowship of his followers.

If true love is not present in your recovery, then true recovery is not happening. You are worthy of love and you are meant to love others. You must be in a place where you are loved in spite of your past. You must also begin to reach out to love others, breaking free from your old ways of selfishness and pride.

GIVE IT ALL AWAY!

The ultimate goal of grace-based recovery is to give away what has been given to you. True recovery transitions you from a life of taking to one of giving, from serving self to serving others. If you are not eventually giving away your recovery, you might need to question whether you have really been recovering.

This area (giving) is where I see the biggest difference between most recovery programs and a grace-based recovery approach. Most recovery programs are self-focused; if you get what you need, you will be whole and happy. But self-centeredness never leads to real peace and fulfillment.

In fact, if you just look at what addiction trains you to do, you will see the fallacy of self-absorption as a means to happiness. Doesn't addiction teach you to make life all about you, taking whatever you want at any cost to ensure that you are "happy"? But the longer you travel that road, the more you realize that it is a false promise. Addiction, and the self-centeredness that underlies it, only lead to emptiness and loneliness. There is no ultimate satisfaction in that!

Grace-based recovery teaches that because you are already loved, valued, and worth recovery, you no longer have to take and take and take to find your happiness. You can finally rest, knowing that your worth is not dependent on how well you have performed for others. You can give love without strings attached because you can never lose the love God has already given you.

And when you learn to embrace grace, you find yourself motivated to help others. You are gaining a soft heart of compassion, no longer bound to your old, hard heart of selfishness. You begin to care because you have experienced care. You show mercy because you have received mercy.

Jesus told the story of a king whose servant owed him more than he could repay in a lifetime. The king wanted to settle the account, so he summoned the servant and said he would be sold, along with his wife and kids, to repay what he owed. But the servant pleaded for mercy, and the king had compassion on him and forgave his debt.

Afterward, this servant went out and found a guy who owed him the barest fraction of what he owed the king. He demanded that the guy pay up. The guy begged for mercy but the servant refused and instead threw him in jail.

When the king found out what the forgiven servant had done, he was furious. The king responded, "You wicked servant! I forgave you all that debt because you pleaded with me. And should not you have had mercy on your fellow servant, as I had mercy on you?" (Matthew 18:32-33).

You cannot be engaged in true recovery without gaining a heart that grows in compassion for others who are struggling just like you have. Grace will compel you to give away to others who desperately need freedom from their own addictions the insight and wisdom you have gained on your journey. This is the only appropriate response to the freedom and kindness God has shown to you.

> People may excite in themselves a glow of compassion, not
> by toasting their feet at the fire, and saying, "Lord, teach me

compassion," but by going and seeking an object that requires compassion. —Henry Ward Beecher

Grace-based recovery is invitational and warm. It is not a place for people to be beaten up further for their foolish mistakes. It is a place for confession, healing, forgiveness, growth, and compassion. It is an environment of multiplying grace upon grace as those who experience healing and growth freely pass along those gifts to those just starting their recovery journey.

Learn to give away your recovery and you will experience joy like you never thought possible. It truly is better to give than to receive!

Leader guide: Go over the discussion questions. Allow your time on Question 5 to set up the group exercise of blessing others. Invite members to do Question 4 as homework.

DISCUSSION QUESTIONS

1. You were made by God to be fully known and fully loved, as well as to know and love others. What makes this difficult to practice?
2. How is love the fundamental opposite of addiction?
3. Why does making life all about yourself never lead to true contentment? Why is sacrificial love essential to joy?
4. Who do you know that could benefit from what you are learning and experiencing in your recovery? What is preventing you from sharing your life with them?
5. What does "It is better to give than to receive" mean to your recovery?

Leader guide: This lesson is all about blessing others through love. Therefore, the group exercise invites members to practice the "art" of blessing one another. Feel free to modify or personalize the blessing as desired, especially if someone in the group does not yet profess faith in Christ. Just ensure that it speaks truth and grace over the individual receiving the blessing. A time of prayer and worship is also encouraged.

Lesson

8

GROUP EXERCISE

Speaking Blessing over Others

To bless others is to speak words of truth and affirmation over them for the purpose of building them up and encouraging them onward. I can think of no better way to conclude this lesson than to spend some time blessing one another.

Each person takes turns being in the middle of a circle. The rest of the group gathers around while one person speaks the following blessing over them. (Laying hands on the person's shoulders or head is encouraged, if this is desired by the person receiving the blessing.)

> [First Name],
>
> We bless you in the name of Jesus Christ. You are a beloved [son/daughter] of the Most High God, created in him to do good works and to be a blessing to others.
>
> You have been given every spiritual blessing in the heavenly realms to fulfill all that God intended for you. Your life is precious to God; therefore it is precious to us.
>
> May you live this day and every day after in the grace and truth of Jesus for the good of others and the sake of his kingdom.
>
> In the power and promises of God, Amen.

Leader guide: Love covers a multitude of sins. Love also is the foundation of grace. So it is fitting that the "end game" of grace-based recovery is to love others. It creates a doorway for those not yet in recovery to find their way into an environment where healing and growth can happen. Reiterate the importance of loving others as a way of "closing the loop" on one's personal recovery. Without love, one gets stuck "in recovery" and misses out on the real joy that the journey is meant to produce.

Wrap up the meeting with prayer and a word of encouragement. And give one final assignment to the group: read the Epilogue and spend some time journaling their thoughts.